SO THAT'S HOW IT WORKS!

ROBOTS AND AI

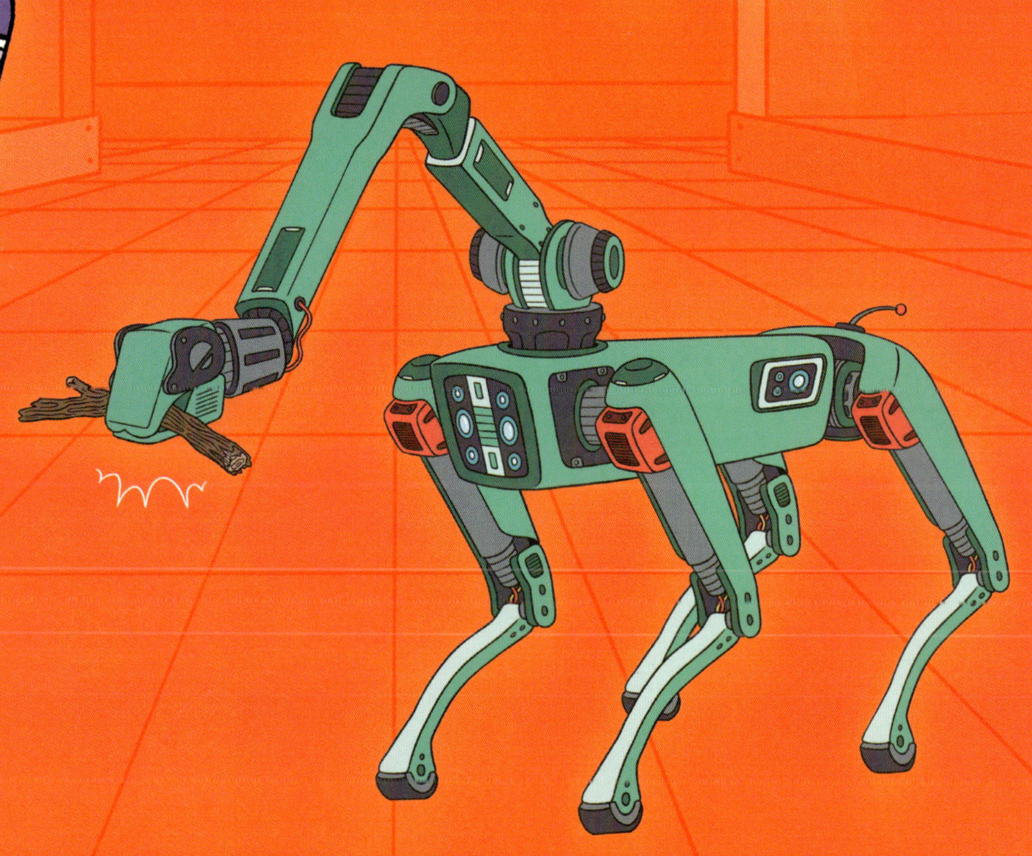

TOM JACKSON • KRISTYNA BACZYNSKI

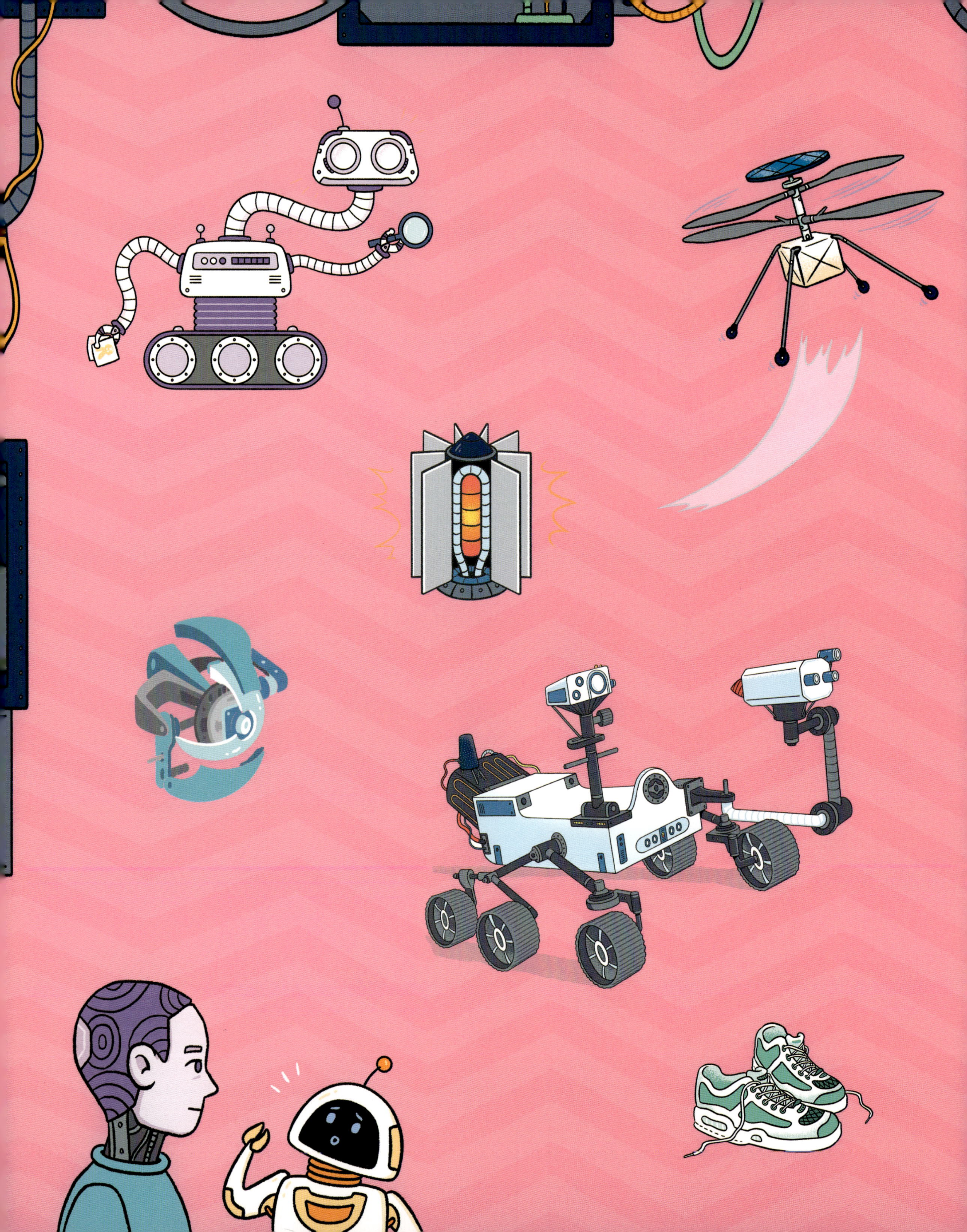

SO THAT'S HOW IT WORKS!

ROBOTS AND AI

HOW ROBOTS AND AI ARE REVOLUTIONISING OUR WORLD

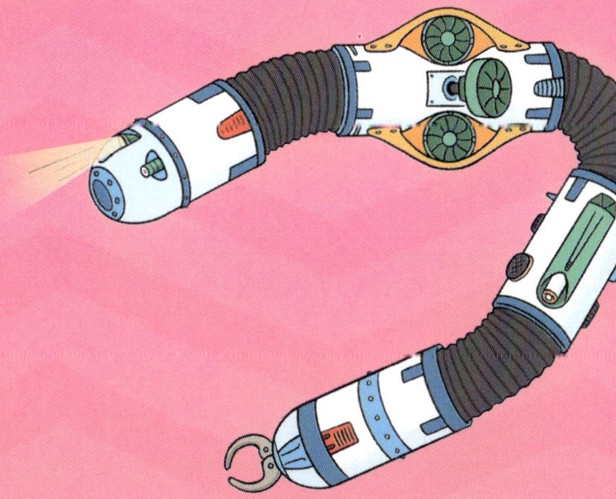

First published 2025 by Kingfisher
an imprint of Macmillan Children's Books
The Smithson, 6 Briset Street, London, EC1M 5NR
Associated companies throughout the world
www.panmacmillan.com

Text by Tom Jackson
Illustrated by Kristyna Baczynski
Consultant Dr Peter Bentley
Edited by Jackie McCann and Paul Virr
Designed by Ariadne Ward and Emily Bornoff

ISBN: 978-0-7534-4871-7

9 8 7 6 5 4 3 2 1
1TR/0525/UG/WKT/128MA

EU representative: Macmillan Publishers Ireland Ltd, 1st Floor, The Liffey Trust Centre, 117-126 Sheriff Street Upper, Dublin 1, D01 YC43

A CIP catalogue record for this book is available from the British Library.

Printed in China

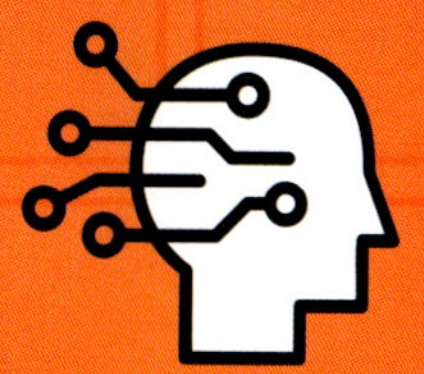

CONTENTS

HELLO ROBOTS!

A robot is a machine that can do a job by itself, once it receives instructions from a human controller or programmer. We call a robot that can do this '**autonomous**'. The robot moves by itself, picks up and carries objects, or builds things automatically. Robots are used in factories and on farms, and by firefighters and doctors, but they mow the lawn and vacuum the carpet too.

ROBOTIC DESIGNS

Robots come in all shapes and sizes, from microscopic **nanobots** to huge robots that can lift a car. Most are constructed using the same basic parts. Some have mechanical arms, legs and other parts, which can make them seem human or animal-like. Robots are more adaptable than other types of machines because they can be programmed to do different jobs.

Alan Turing

Alan Turing, a British mathematician, laid the foundations for computer science in 1936. He wondered if machines could think like humans and, in 1950, designed the 'Turing Test', where a person talks to a machine and a human, without knowing which is which. If the person can't tell the difference, the machine passes the test. This idea led to the field of **artificial intelligence**, which enables computers to think and learn more like us.

ROBOTS AND AI

MOST ROBOTS ARE PROGRAMMABLE MACHINES THAT FOLLOW INSTRUCTIONS, BUT THERE ARE A FEW ROBOTS THAT ARE MORE INDEPENDENT AND CAN FIGURE OUT WHAT TO DO WITHOUT A HUMAN AT THE CONTROLS.

SOME VERY SPECIALISED ROBOTS USE ARTIFICIAL INTELLIGENCE, OR AI, WHICH ALLOWS THEM TO LEARN AND MAKE THEIR OWN DECISIONS.

A HUMAN CONTROLLER HAS GIVEN THE ROVER A TASK: TO FIND WATER ON MARS. THE ROBOT ROVER'S AI ALLOWS IT TO DECIDE IF A PLACE IS WORTH INVESTIGATING, AND WHICH SCIENTIFIC INSTRUMENTS TO USE.

The tool at the end of a robot arm that allows it to do a job is called an **end effector**. This is a gripper tool, for holding things.

AI CAN SPOT FACES IN PICTURES, READ AND WRITE STORIES, CREATE VIDEOS, OR MAKE MEDICINES. IT HELPS ROBOTS TO DO JOBS BY THEMSELVES, SUCH AS DRIVING CARS.

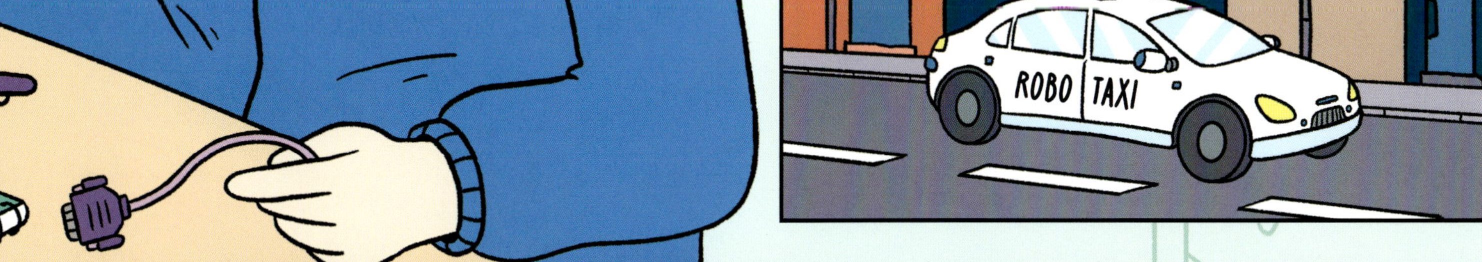

FACTORY ROBOT

Robots are hard at work in factories all over the world, including car factories. A robotic arm is a robot that tackles all kinds of difficult and repetitive jobs, from assembling parts, to welding metal, and painting bodywork. The design of this mechanical worker is based on the human arm, but much stronger.

MAKING MOVES

A robotic arm has six 'joints', allowing it to move in six separate ways at the same time. Each joint is called an **axis of movement** and is controlled by an **actuator,** so each one can move independently. In this robotic arm the actuators are electric motors called **stepper motors**. They are controlled by a computer, which coordinates all the motors so the arm moves in the correct way.

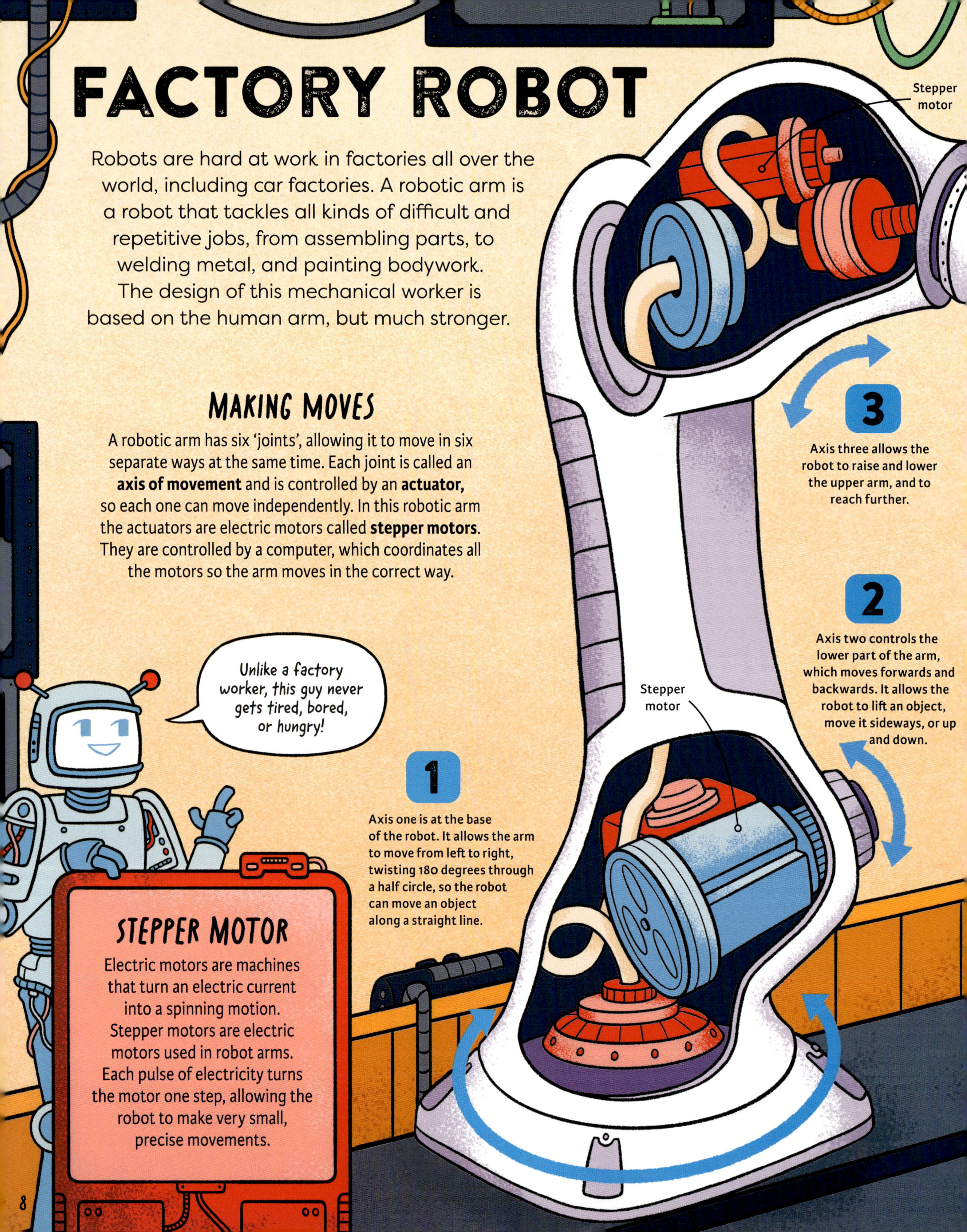

STEPPER MOTOR

Electric motors are machines that turn an electric current into a spinning motion. Stepper motors are electric motors used in robot arms. Each pulse of electricity turns the motor one step, allowing the robot to make very small, precise movements.

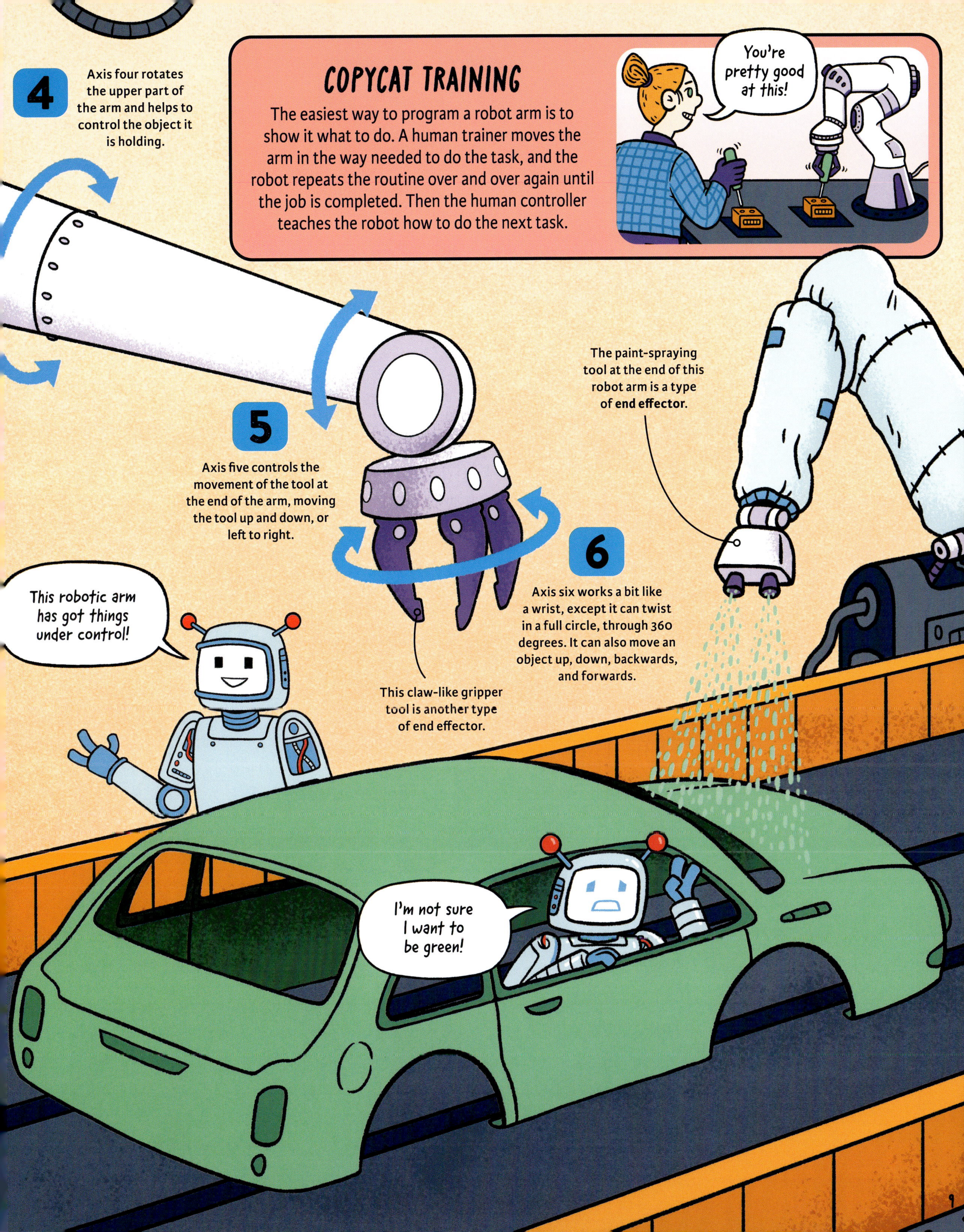
4
Axis four rotates the upper part of the arm and helps to control the object it is holding.
COPYCAT TRAINING
The easiest way to program a robot arm is to show it what to do. A human trainer moves the arm in the way needed to do the task, and the robot repeats the routine over and over again until the job is completed. Then the human controller teaches the robot how to do the next task.
You're pretty good at this!
The paint-spraying tool at the end of this robot arm is a type of end effector.
5
Axis five controls the movement of the tool at the end of the arm, moving the tool up and down, or left to right.
6
Axis six works a bit like a wrist, except it can twist in a full circle, through 360 degrees. It can also move an object up, down, backwards, and forwards.
This robotic arm has got things under control!
This claw-like gripper tool is another type of end effector.
I'm not sure I want to be green!

ROBOT GRIPPERS

When the end of a robot arm is fitted with an **end effector**, the robot can do all kinds of jobs. Some end effectors are shaped like robotic hands with 'fingers'. Lifting and holding things seems easy to us with our amazing hands, but for robots, it isn't so simple.

Nice moves robot buddy!

This gripper pushes outwards to lift the cup.

This gripper pushes inwards, to lift the cup

Each finger on the gripper has a **sensor,** which measures how hard it pushes on the object. It stops pushing when the force is great enough.

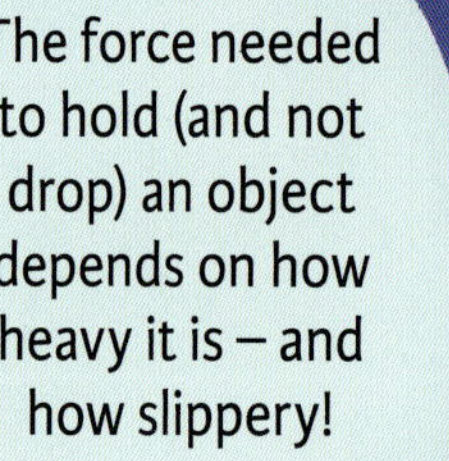

The force needed to hold (and not drop) an object depends on how heavy it is – and how slippery!

This end effector has more fingers, for better grip.

The force for gripping a potato is not the same as the force needed for picking up a strawberry.

The gripper uses a different technique for picking up fragile objects. Each finger can move on its own, just like human fingers.

GET A GRIP

Robot grippers work in different ways to suit different jobs. They might allow a robot to pick up objects that are small and light, heavy and bulky, or fragile and delicate.

SUCTION

Suckers pick up flat objects, such as boxes.

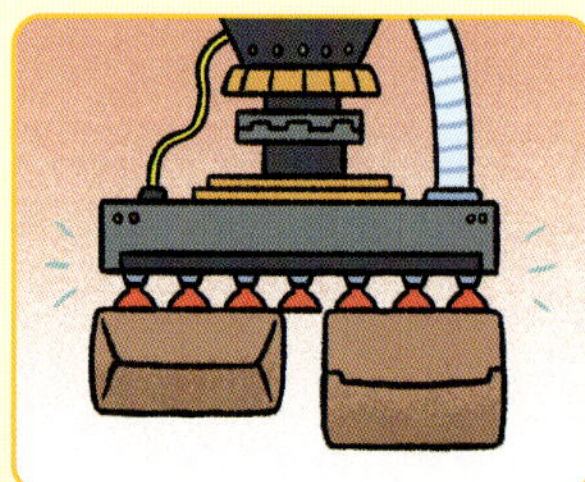

ELECTROSTATIC

An electric charge can make objects stick together, like a party balloon sticks to your sweater.

MAGNETIC

Electromagnets pick up steel and other metals containing iron.

ROBOT GRIPPERS IN SPACE

The International Space Station (ISS) is a research station that orbits Earth. Attached to the ISS is a long robotic arm called Canadarm 2, which has a large, hand-like attachment called **Dextre**, or Canada Hand. Together, they are two of the most advanced space robots ever built.

DEXTRE

Dextre is fitted with five cameras, which astronauts use to monitor the ISS and to watch supply ships coming and going. There are no jobs too tough for Dextre – it can hold and work with equipment as small as a toaster or as big as a fridge.

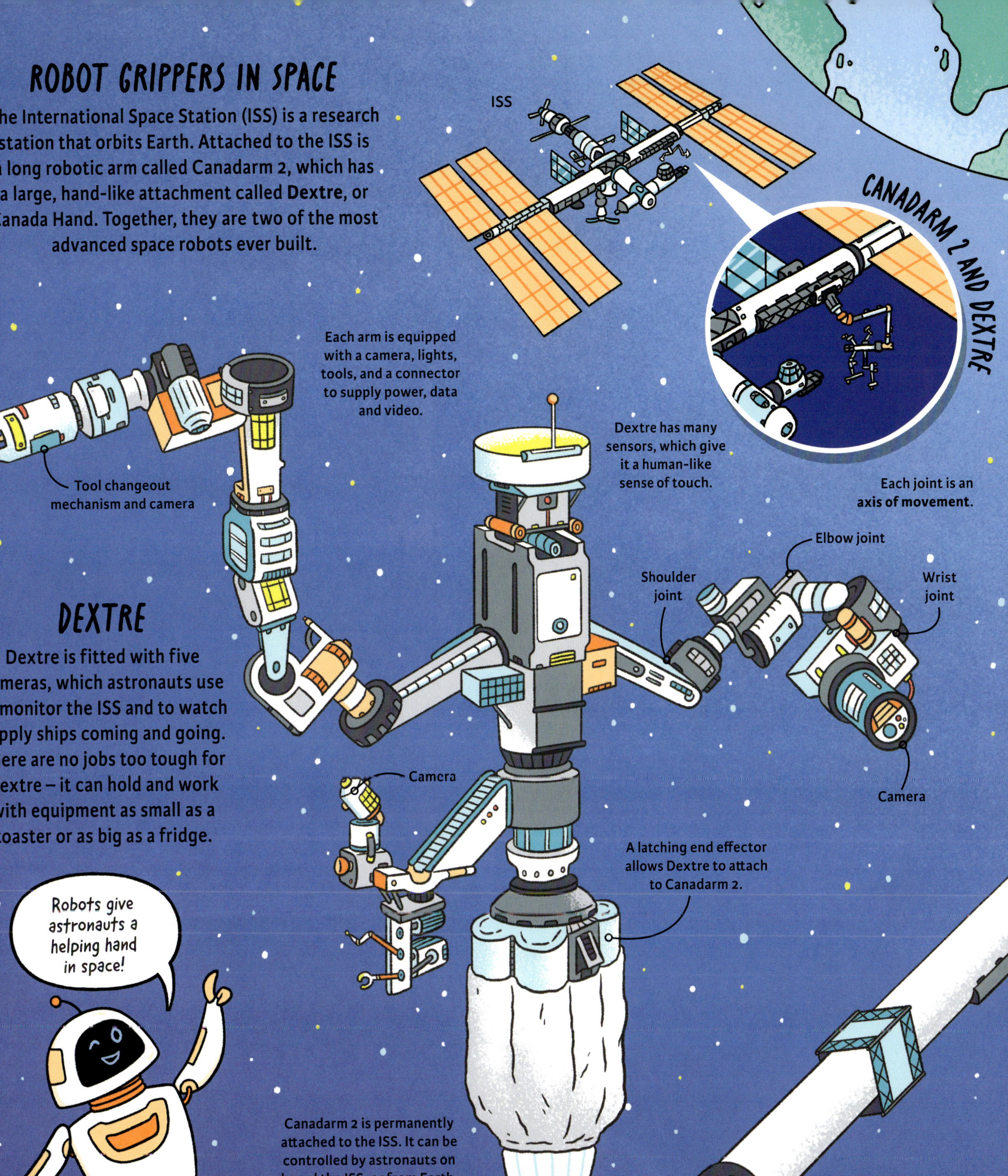

FIREFIGHTING ROBOTS

Firefighting is a dangerous job that requires great skill and courage. When a fire breaks out and the temperature soars, there may be toxic fumes, dense smoke, and buildings on the verge of collapse. In this situation, robot firefighters are indispensable.

It's an emergency, the building's on fire! It's too dangerous to send people inside – this is a job for a firefighting robot.

A FIREFIGHTING ROBOT IS BUILT LIKE AN ARMOURED TANK. THE BODY IS MADE OF ALUMINIUM AND STEEL, TO PROTECT THE CONTROL SYSTEMS AND ENGINE FROM HEAT, SMOKE, AND FALLING OBJECTS.

THE ROBOT DRIVES ON CATERPILLAR TRACKS. THEY GRIP ROUGH GROUND AND DRIVE UP STEEP SLOPES - EVEN HOLES IN THE ROAD WON'T STOP THIS FIREFIGHTER.

FIREFIGHTERS CAN LOCATE A FIRE IN A SMOKE-FILLED BUILDING, BECAUSE THE ROBOT HAS AN INFRARED CAMERA THAT CAN DETECT HEAT, EVEN THROUGH THE WALLS.

INTO A FIERY VOLCANO

Some places are too hot even for firefighting robots. In 1994, a robot called Dante II crawled into an active volcano in Alaska, USA, and made its way down into the smoking crater. Its mission? To help scientists develop technology for space exploration.

Secured tether stabilises Dante II from behind.

A laser scanner sweeps the area, measuring distance.

A tilt camera sways to allow a steady view.

Different **sensors** measure incline, direction and levels of toxic gases.

Leg **actuators** move independently, to adjust position and avoid obstacles.

Video cameras are used for navigation and science.

Dante II

Dante II was fitted with cameras and sensors to measure hot gases and smoke. At first, the robot was controlled remotely by operators. Later, it operated semi-**autonomously**, sending data back to the controller via satellite. Dante II made it to the bottom of the volcano, but fell over on its way out and couldn't be rescued.

FLYING DRONE

A **drone** is a flying machine that is controlled from the ground, which makes it a type of **remote operated vehicle (ROV)**. However, a drone can also run **autonomously** if it needs to, including during the take-off and landing, so it is also a type of flying robot.

A BIRD'S-EYE VIEW

Drones fitted with cameras can give us a bird's-eye-view of the ground from high in the air. Film-makers use them to shoot scenes, while farmers use them to check their herds and crops. Powerful drones can deliver packages to remote places in emergencies.

Half of the propellers spin in one direction, the other half spin in the opposite direction. This stops the drone from whizzing around in a circle, keeping it stable.

The drone sends and receives radio signals via the antenna.

The electronic speed control (ESC) makes micro adjustments to the power, so the propeller motors can steer the drone and keep it flying. Each propeller has its own ESC.

Powerful battery

CONTROLLER

The controller on the ground sends signals that steer the drone. The camera on the drone sends back a live video feed, giving the controller a first person view – as if they were sitting inside the drone.

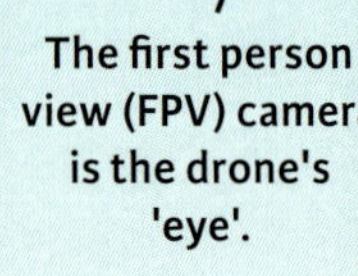

The first person view (FPV) camera is the drone's 'eye'.

Landing gear allows the drone to stand on the ground.

SATELLITE NAVIGATION

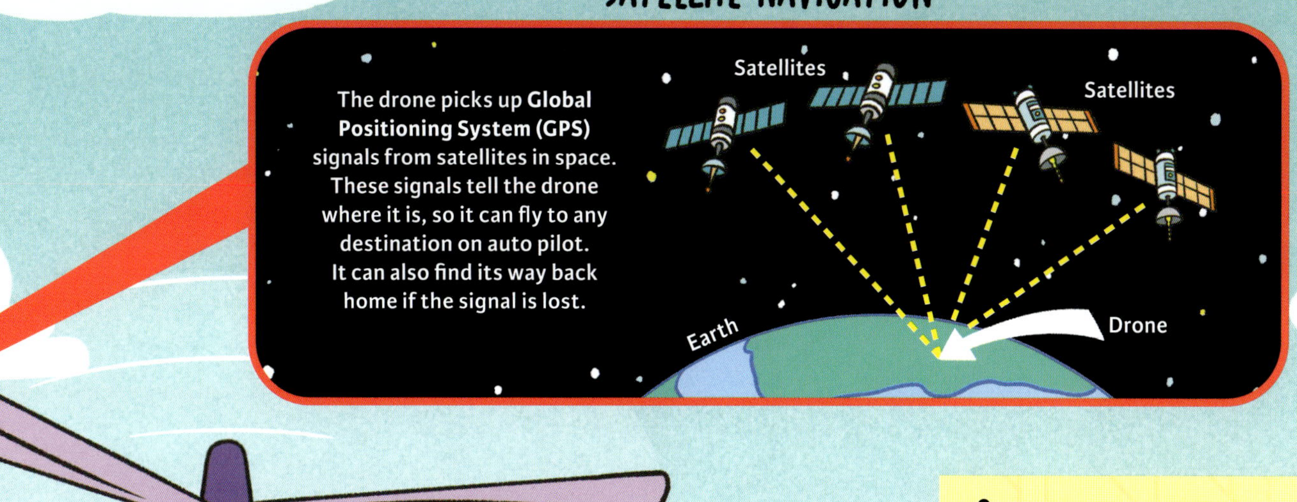

The **actuators** on this robot are standard propellers. They have wing-shaped blades that pull the drone into the air as they spin.

The flight controller is a small computer controlling the camera and steering system. It automatically adjusts the speed of each propeller, keeping the drone in the air, even in a strong wind.

Propeller motor

The hub is the central unit holding the cameras, battery and antennas.

Drone Swarms

With the help of **AI**, drones no longer need constant human control and can operate with more **autonomy**.

A fleet of drones can move as one unit, like a flock of birds or a swarm of bees. The flying robots communicate with each other using AI. They analyse data in real time and coordinate movements to avoid mid-air collisions.

Drone swarms could be used to fight wildfires or detect diseases in crops. The downside is they could also be used to spy, or for warfare.

Hundreds of small light drones can create dazzling light displays in the night sky.

MECH SUITS

A mech suit, or **exoskeleton**, is like a wearable robot – a robotic body controlled by the person inside it. The robotics make the wearer stronger, so they can do jobs that require more strength than that of an average human being.

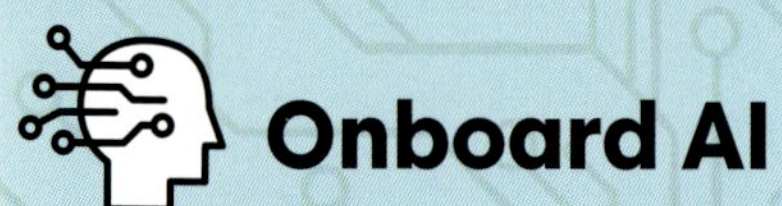

Onboard AI

There are **sensors** in the feet, knees and hips that help the mech suit match the rhythm of the wearer.

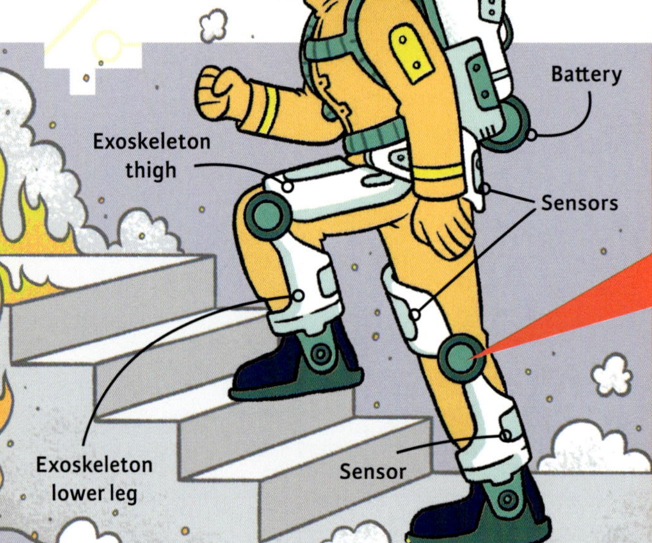

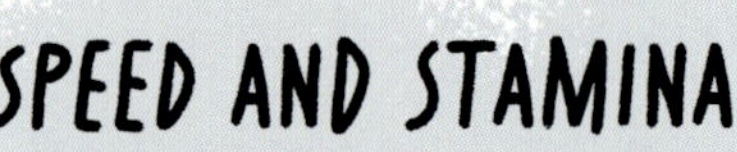

SPEED AND STAMINA

This lightweight mech suit is fitted to the operator's lower body and is jointed at the legs and feet. Its **actuators** allow the wearer to walk at speed for long periods of time.

POWERED KNEE JOINT

The hip, knee and ankle joints of the mech suit are powered by electric motors. When a limb moves, the motors match and boost the strength of the wearer's movements.

HEAVY-WEIGHT POWER

A full-body mech suit gives the wearer super strength, so they can lift and carry heavy loads safely. These robotic systems are designed for demanding jobs in factories, farming, and on building sites.

To move the suit, the wearer pulls triggers in the hand controllers. Sensors pick up the wearer's arm and leg movements. Motors move the heavy-duty suit to match the wearer's movements.

GRIPPERS AND OTHER TYPES OF END EFFECTOR HOOK ON TO THE GRAB HANDLES.

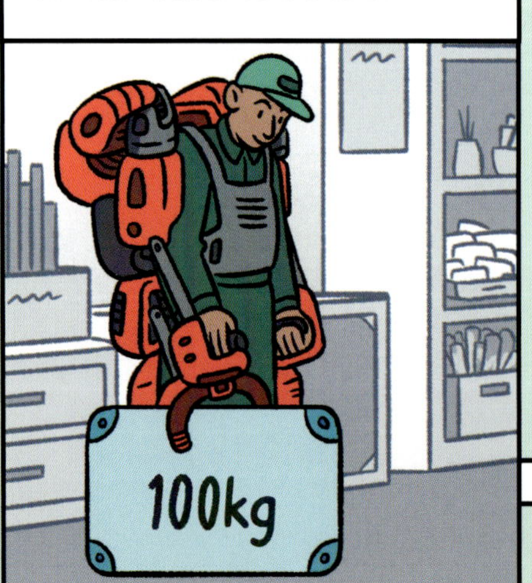

AN EXOSKELETON CAN INCREASE A USER'S STRENGTH BY 20 TIMES!

MEDICAL MARVEL

Mech suits are being developed for people who are paralysed and cannot move their arms or legs. They also help patients who have severe injuries or diseases that impair movement.

THINK, ACTION!

Sensors on the surface of the brain allow the wearer to control a mech suit or a wheelchair with only their thoughts! One day, electrodes deep in the brain vessels may replace sensors.

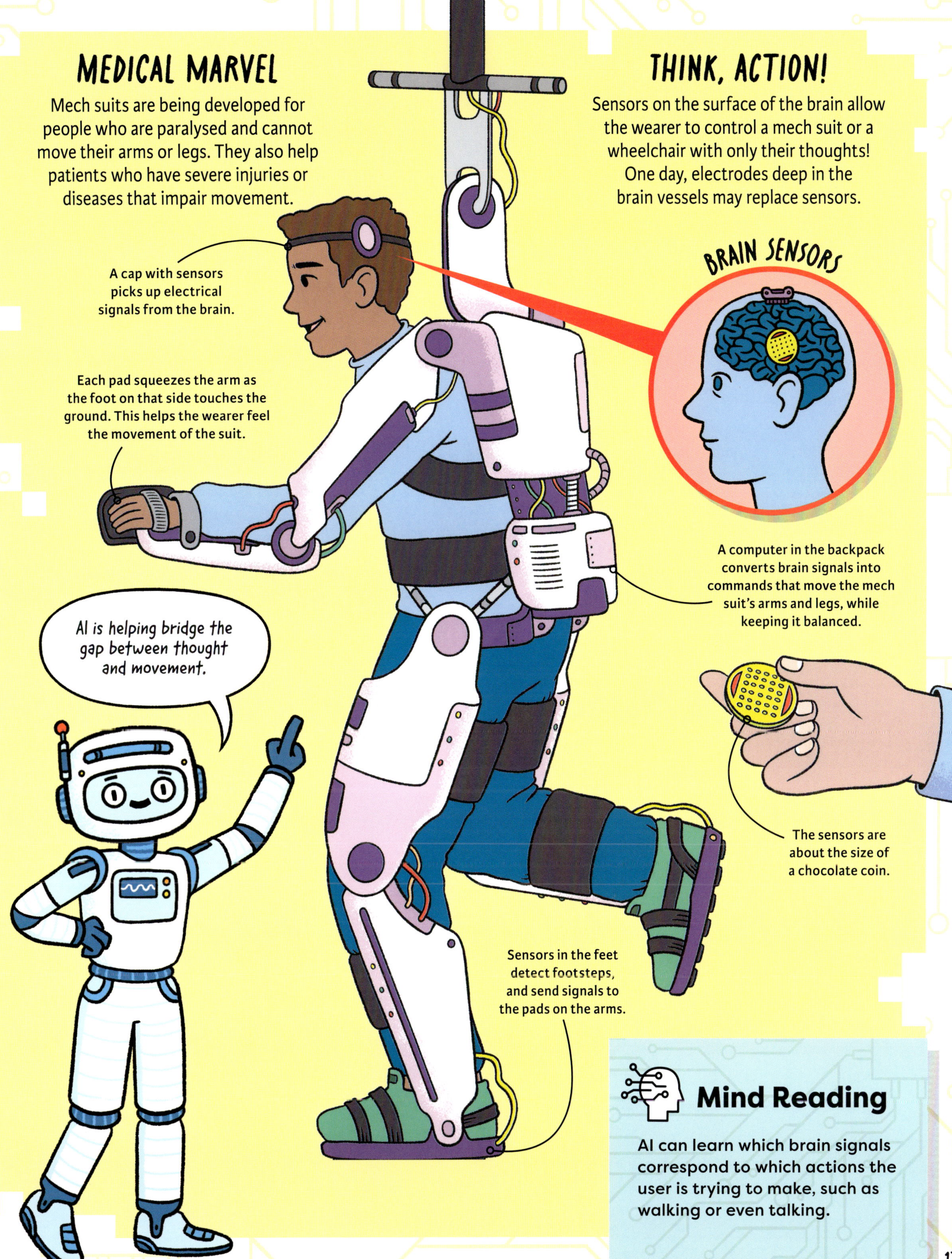

Mind Reading

AI can learn which brain signals correspond to which actions the user is trying to make, such as walking or even talking.

TELEPRESENCE ROBOT

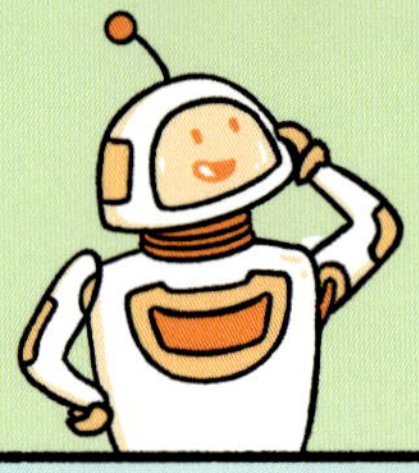

Imagine being able to visit far-off places without travelling anywhere. You could go on a work trip or to a party, and meet new people without leaving your home. All you need is a telepresence robot!

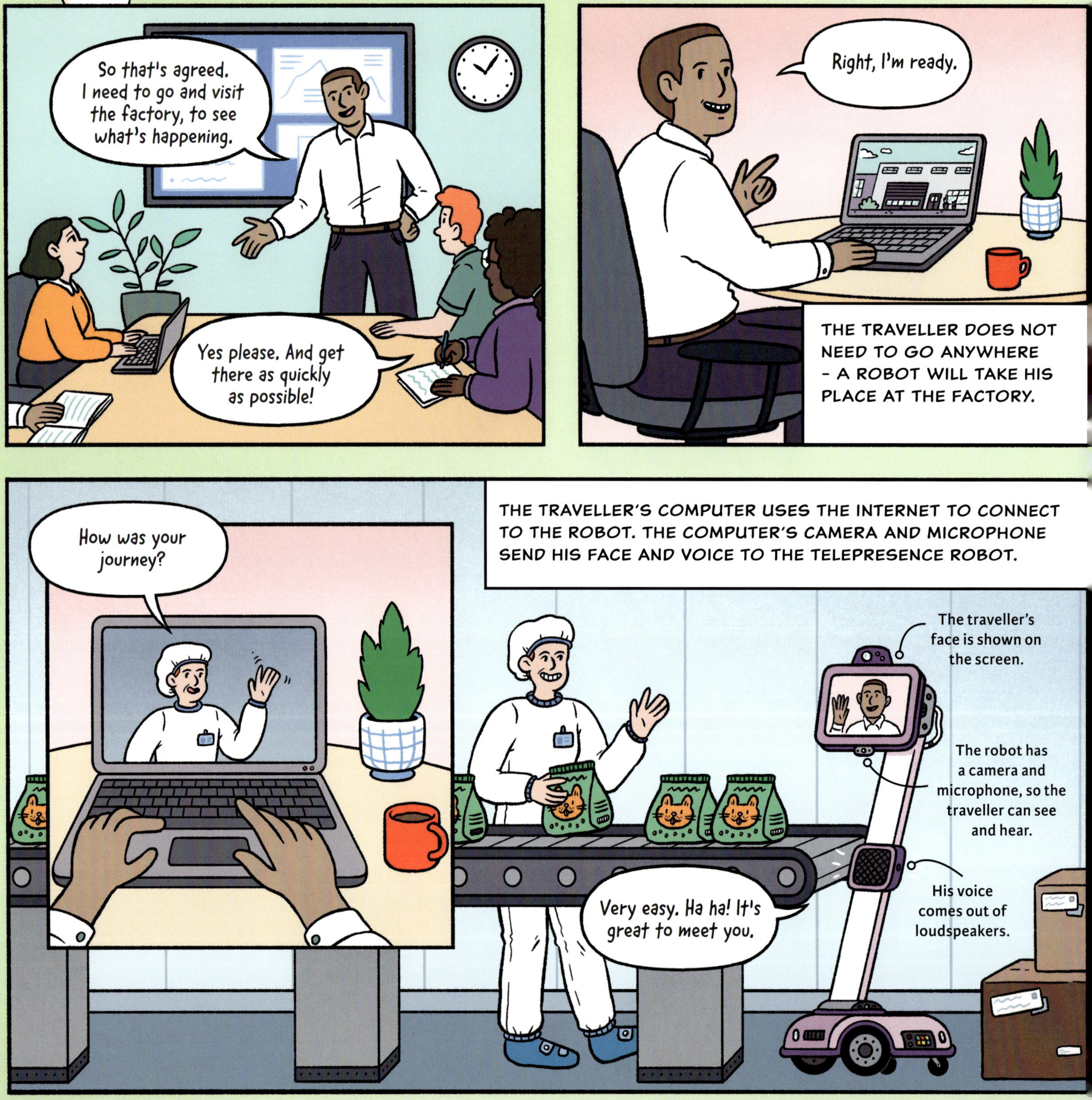

THE TRAVELLER'S COMPUTER USES THE INTERNET TO CONNECT TO THE ROBOT. THE COMPUTER'S CAMERA AND MICROPHONE SEND HIS FACE AND VOICE TO THE TELEPRESENCE ROBOT.

How was your journey?

Very easy. Ha ha! It's great to meet you.

The traveller's face is shown on the screen.

The robot has a camera and microphone, so the traveller can see and hear.

His voice comes out of loudspeakers.

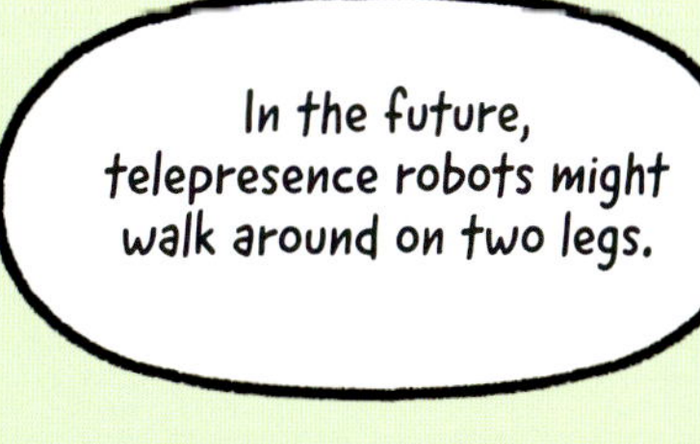

Using virtual reality

One way to make the telepresence robot even better is to add virtual reality (VR). A VR headset can give the traveller a clearer view of where their robot is, and show things in 3D, so it seems just like the real world. The telepresence robot would use a 360-degree camera to video everything in the area at once. The traveller could then look around just by turning their head.

FRIENDLY ROBOTS

Androids and humanoids are robots designed to work closely with people. A humanoid robot will probably have a head, arms and legs, but it still looks like a robot. An android is designed to look like a human being, with realistic facial expressions and the ability to speak. Let's take a look...

ANDROID ROBOTS COPY HUMAN MOVEMENTS AND GESTURES, SO THEY CAN WORK AND INTERACT CLOSELY WITH HUMANS.

MECHANICAL SHOULDER AND ARM JOINTS ALLOW THESE ROBOTS TO COPY HUMAN MOVEMENTS. THE FINGERS ON THEIR HANDS MOVE SEPARATELY, ALLOWING THEM TO POINT AND GESTURE.

ADVANCED FACIAL EXPRESSIONS AND HAND GESTURES ALLOW ANDROID ROBOTS TO EXPRESS MORE INFORMATION.

ANDROID FACES CAN BE CONVINCINGLY LIFE-LIKE.

HOW IT WORKS

Built-in sensors allow android and humanoid robots to track movement across a room and turn to face people. These robots are equipped with face and voice recognition, and can detect different emotions and ages, which helps them respond in an appropriate way.

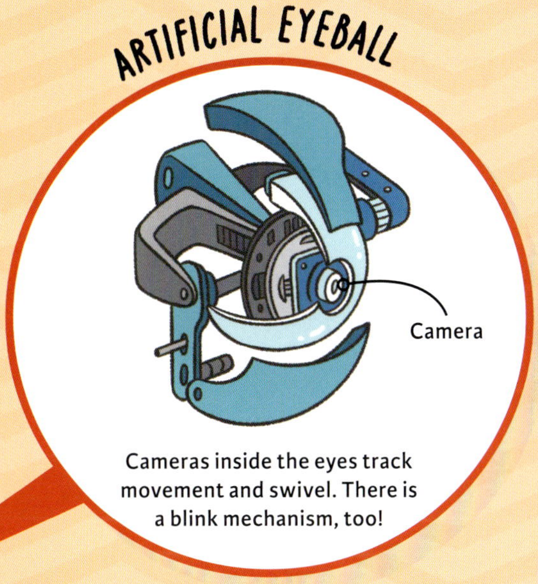

Levers and gears behind the face push or pull to create a smile or a frown.

Eyebrows wiggle up and down.

ARTIFICIAL EYEBALL

Camera

Cameras inside the eyes track movement and swivel. There is a blink mechanism, too!

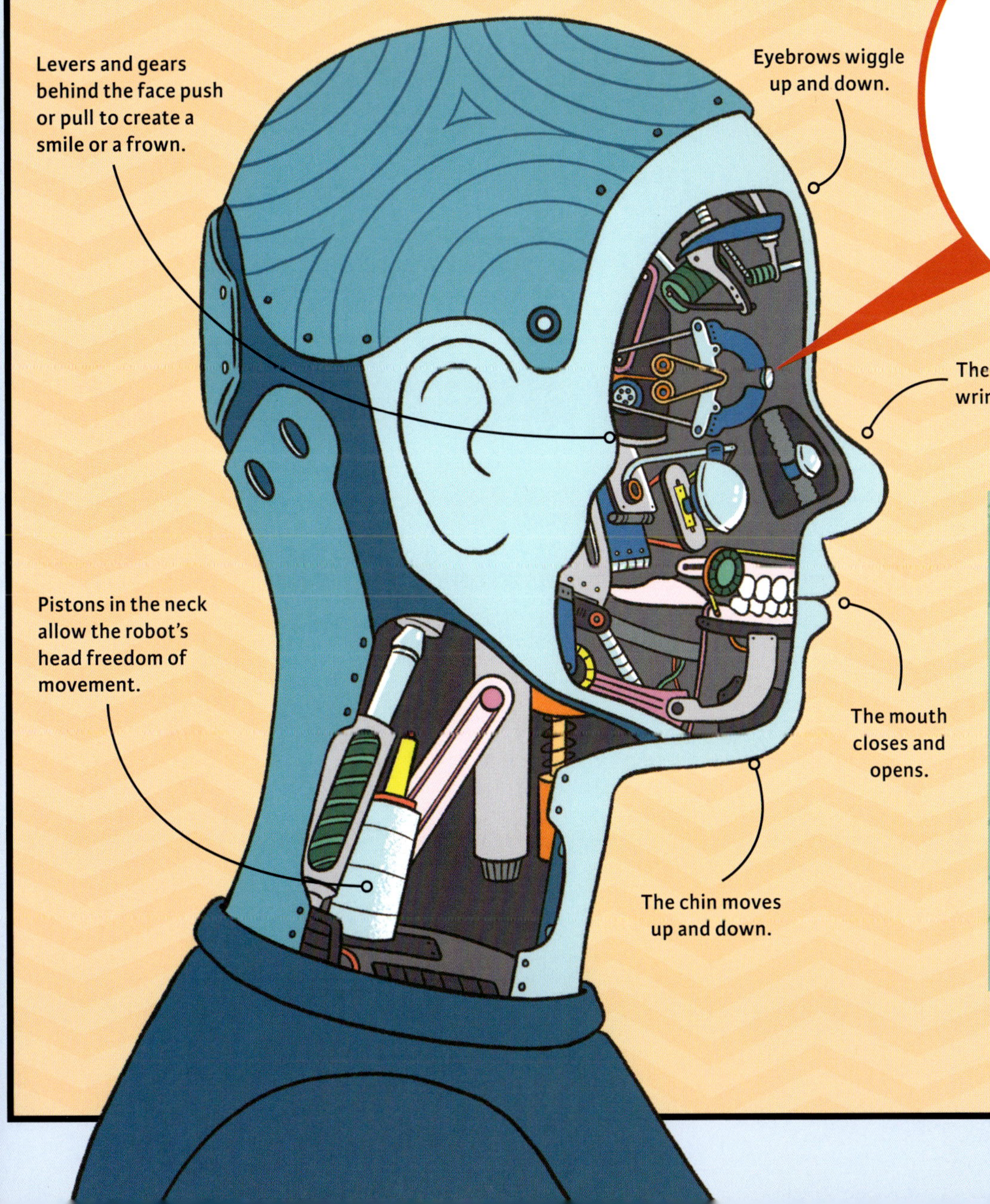

The nose wrinkles.

Pistons in the neck allow the robot's head freedom of movement.

The mouth closes and opens.

The chin moves up and down.

Self Teaching

Engineers are using AI to develop androids that imitate humans even more convincingly. But it's still a challenge to build robots that walk and talk like us. In the future, humanoid and android robots will be able to teach themselves how to react to their environment, working alongside people and interracting with us.

ROBO-DOG

Building a robot that walks on two legs like a human is complicated for robot designers. A simpler and more practical solution for a stable and agile robot is to give it four legs, like a dog. The latest robot 'dogs' move quickly over rough ground and climb stairs, while carrying tools that allow them to do a variety of jobs.

WORKING DOG

A robot dog is designed to move about, carrying tools that it can put to good use. It's powered by a rechargeable battery, and an onboard computer with **AI** co-ordinates the robot's movements, so that it can walk, run, jump, and climb stairs. **Actuators** in the hip and knee joints allow it to move.

A mechanical arm is mounted on the robot's back.

The **end effector** is a pincer-like gripper that can grasp an object or open doors.

Forward facing cameras work together like a pair of human eyes, so the robot can detect objects and work out how far away they are.

Tough plastic armour keeps out dust and rain.

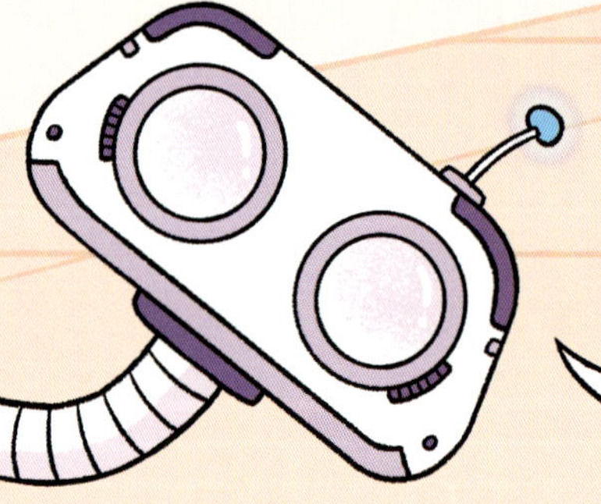

A Giant Leap

AI software is improving robot dogs all the time. AI enables them to figure out the best way to tackle obstacles through a process of trial and error. This makes them more **autonomous**, which means they can work without a human controller.

WHEN IT COMES TO PATROLLING FACTORIES OR INDUSTRIAL FACILITIES ROBOT DOGS ARE IDEAL. THEY HAVE ALL-ROUND VISION AND NEVER NEED A BREAK. THIS MAKES THEM AN ASSET ON SEARCH AND RESCUE MISSIONS TOO.

ROBOT DOGS ARE AGILE. THEY MOVE IN A NUMBER OF WAYS, JUST LIKE REAL DOGS.

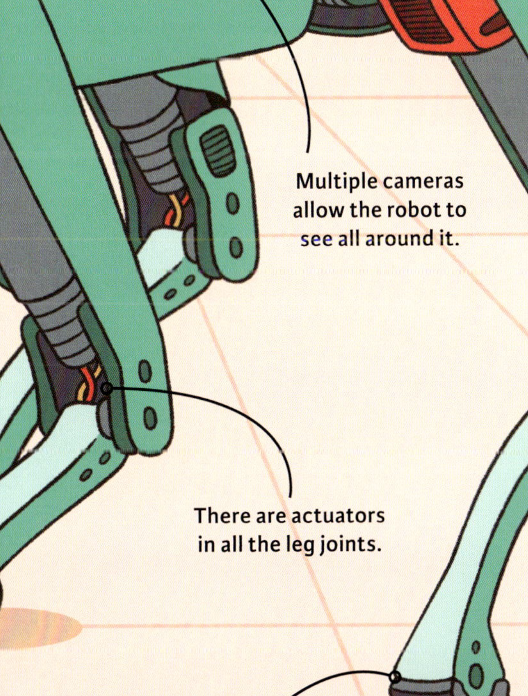

Robo-dog has video cameras, infrared cameras (to pick up heat signals), **lidar** scanners (to map the surrounding area), and hazard detectors.

Actuators in the legs are **hydraulic pistons**, which act like super strong muscles. They allow the robot to push, pull, or press in one direction, with a lot of force.

Small feet make it easier to stand on rough ground. Robo-dog's paws are covered in rough rubber, for extra grip on smooth surfaces.

HYDRAULIC PISTONS

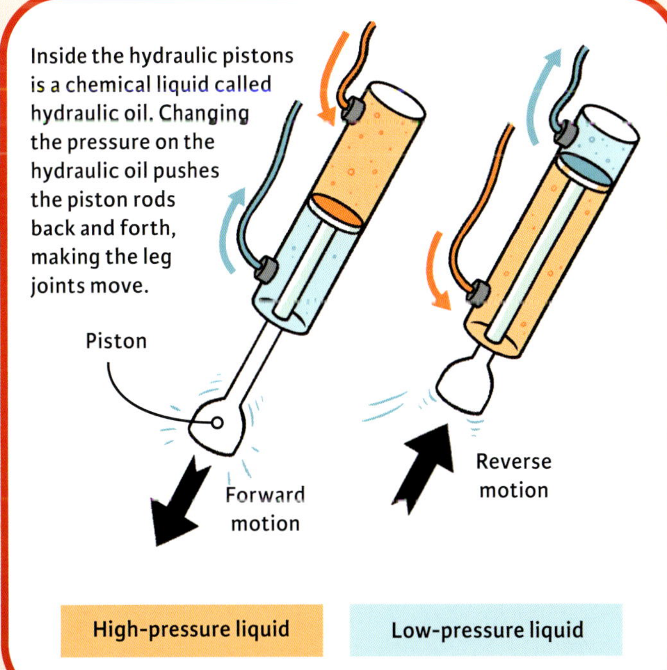

ROBOT VACUUM

Robots don't mind doing household chores - they'll even clean your floor! A robot vacuum cleaner uses sensors and AI features to move around your house, cleaning the floors automatically. It can keep the floors clean while you're asleep, or even if you're away.

The robot recharges at a docking station.

I don't have a flat body shape, so that's one less chore for me!

A **lidar** sensor measures distance, helping AI map the room and deciding a path for the robot.

A flat, low body shape allows this robot vacuum to clean under furniture.

Wheels underneath are driven by electric motors, which work with movement sensors to figure out how far the robot has moved.

A small spinning side brush extends beyond the round body, sweeping up dust from the edges of walls and furniture.

Cameras take pictures of fixed objects in your home, to help the robot remember the walls, furniture, and route back to the docking station.

HAZARD WARNING!

Electric cables and shoe laces can get caught in the brushes or wheels of a robot vacuum. Cameras and image recognition software powered by AI help vacuum robots to identify and avoid these hazards.

Making Maps

A robot vacuum cleaner is an **autonomous** robot, which means it works by itself, without a human in control. The robot maps the shape and size of the room. It uses its lidar sensor to beam out invisible lasers, which reflect off walls and furniture. With help from AI, the robot works out the best cleaning route from the signals it receives, mapping as it goes.

Sensors

The robot uses sensors to continuously check its position against the map it has made. The onboard AI processes the signals, and tells the robot vacuum how to react and how to avoid obstacles.

Bump

The front bumper is a touch sensor, which tells the robot if it has bumped into something. The robot updates its internal map and knows not to get so close next time!

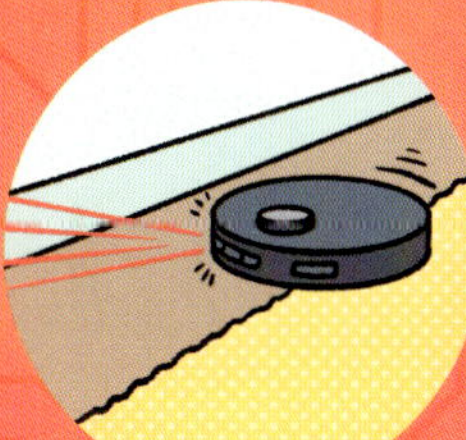

Cliff

An infrared sensor under the robot is always looking at the floor. If there is a sudden drop and the robot cannot detect the ground, it stops immediately. Otherwise, it might tumble down the stairs!

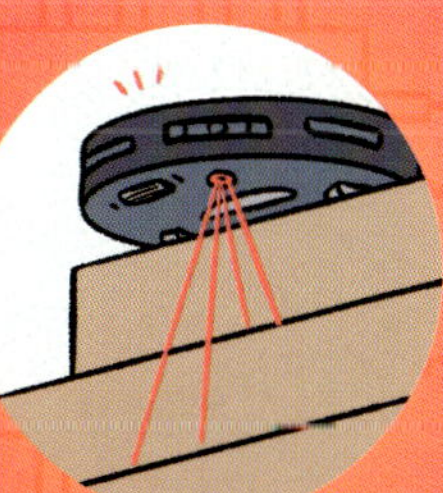

Floor tracking

These sensors pick up a change in floor surface, such as carpet to wood. The robot adjusts the brushes and power of the vacuum to suit.

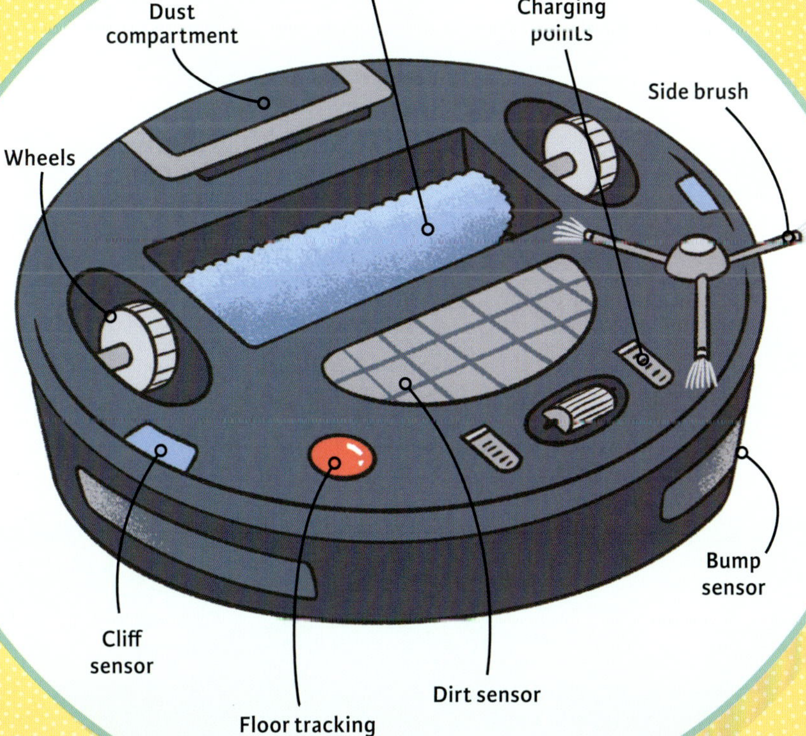

SMART HOME

More and more of the gadgets in our home connect to the Internet. This means we can control them from far away, using an app on our phone. It also means that the gadgets are connected to one other. This is known as the Internet of Things – most of the activity comes from gadgets, or "things", not from people. The "things" use AI to decide what to do, and the result is a smart home that can run all by itself.

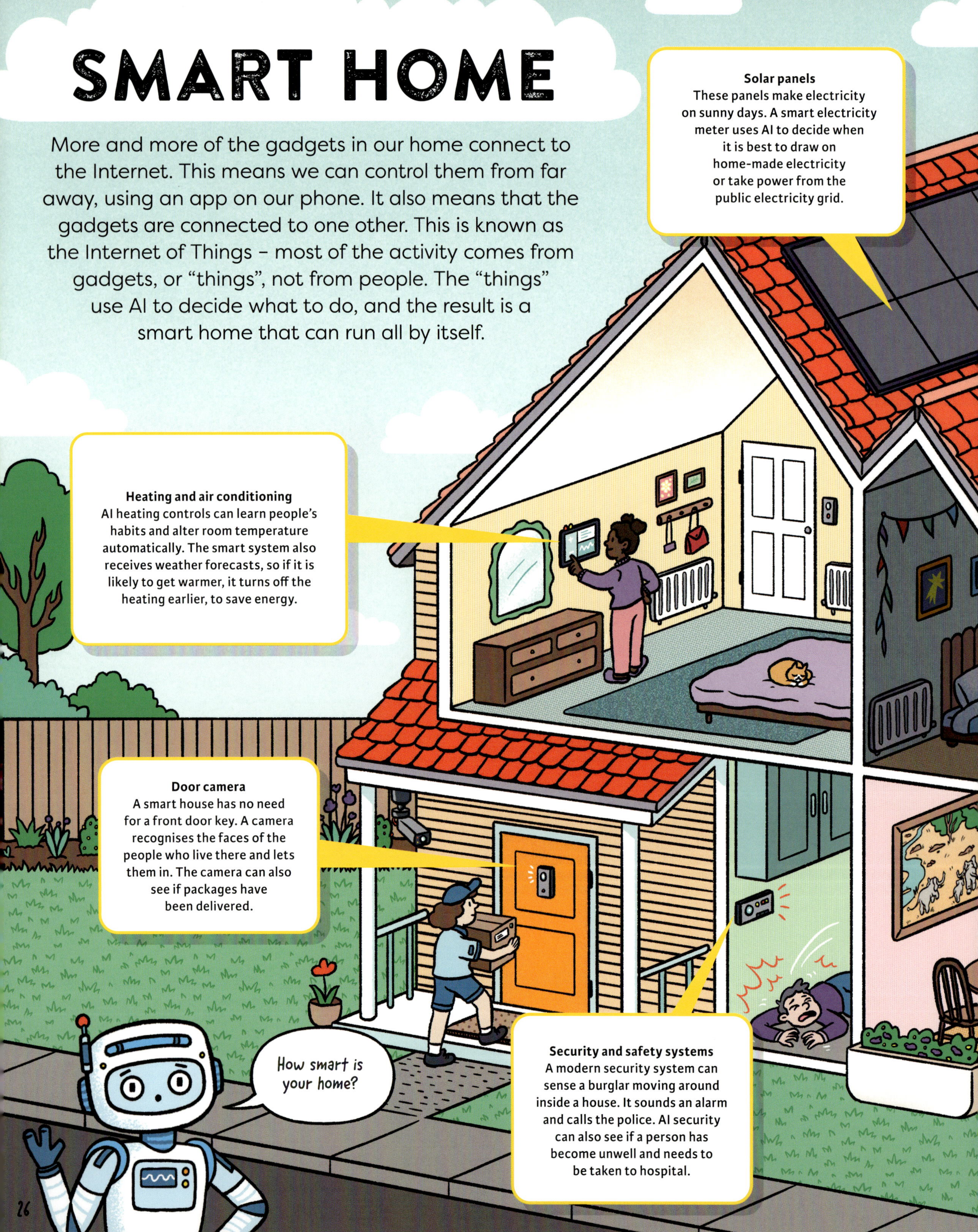

Solar panels
These panels make electricity on sunny days. A smart electricity meter uses AI to decide when it is best to draw on home-made electricity or take power from the public electricity grid.

Heating and air conditioning
AI heating controls can learn people's habits and alter room temperature automatically. The smart system also receives weather forecasts, so if it is likely to get warmer, it turns off the heating earlier, to save energy.

Door camera
A smart house has no need for a front door key. A camera recognises the faces of the people who live there and lets them in. The camera can also see if packages have been delivered.

Security and safety systems
A modern security system can sense a burglar moving around inside a house. It sounds an alarm and calls the police. AI security can also see if a person has become unwell and needs to be taken to hospital.

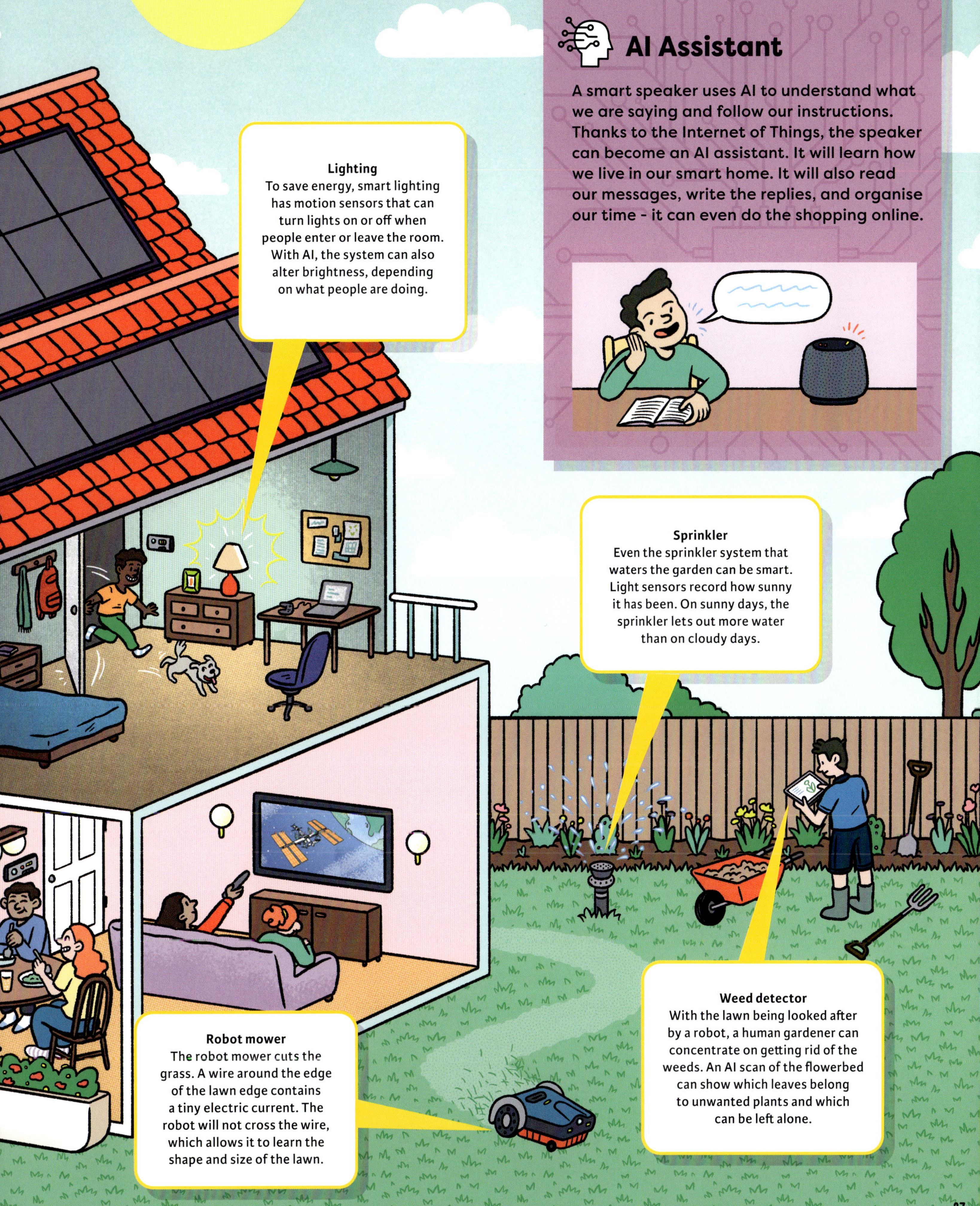

AI Assistant

A smart speaker uses AI to understand what we are saying and follow our instructions. Thanks to the Internet of Things, the speaker can become an AI assistant. It will learn how we live in our smart home. It will also read our messages, write the replies, and organise our time - it can even do the shopping online.

Lighting
To save energy, smart lighting has motion sensors that can turn lights on or off when people enter or leave the room. With AI, the system can also alter brightness, depending on what people are doing.

Sprinkler
Even the sprinkler system that waters the garden can be smart. Light sensors record how sunny it has been. On sunny days, the sprinkler lets out more water than on cloudy days.

Weed detector
With the lawn being looked after by a robot, a human gardener can concentrate on getting rid of the weeds. An AI scan of the flowerbed can show which leaves belong to unwanted plants and which can be left alone.

Robot mower
The robot mower cuts the grass. A wire around the edge of the lawn edge contains a tiny electric current. The robot will not cross the wire, which allows it to learn the shape and size of the lawn.

A driverless car is a rolling robot that plans a route and drives passengers from A to B all by itself. A computer with onboard **AI** controls the steering, brakes and speed. At the same time, the car's AI uses **sensors** to take in information about its surroundings, and is ready to react immediately.

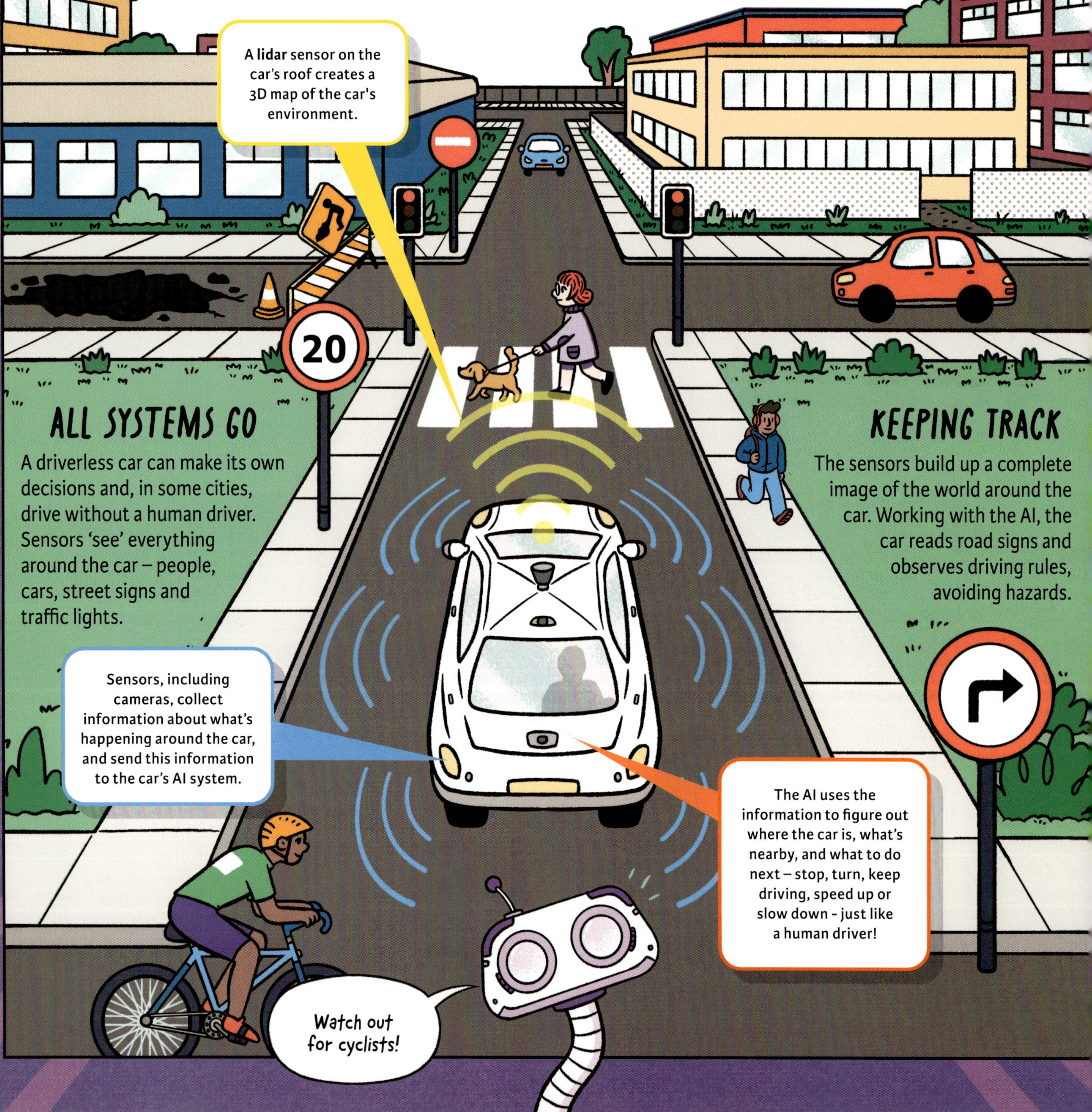

A **lidar** sensor on the car's roof creates a 3D map of the car's environment.

20

ALL SYSTEMS GO

A driverless car can make its own decisions and, in some cities, drive without a human driver. Sensors 'see' everything around the car – people, cars, street signs and traffic lights.

KEEPING TRACK

The sensors build up a complete image of the world around the car. Working with the AI, the car reads road signs and observes driving rules, avoiding hazards.

Sensors, including cameras, collect information about what's happening around the car, and send this information to the car's AI system.

The AI uses the information to figure out where the car is, what's nearby, and what to do next – stop, turn, keep driving, speed up or slow down - just like a human driver!

Watch out for cyclists!

SOME CARS USE AI TO HELP WITH DIRECTIONS OR PARKING, BUT A DRIVER IS STILL AT THE WHEEL AND IN CONTROL. HERE, CAMERAS DETECT OBJECTS AROUND THE CAR AND FEED INFORMATION BACK TO THE AI.

THE AI SYSTEM LETS THE DRIVER KNOW IF THE CAR IS ABOUT TO COLLIDE WITH AN OBJECT IT IS MOVING TOWARDS. IT MAY APPLY BRAKES TO AVOID A COLLISION.

MODERN CARS ARE FITTED WITH **GPS**, A NAVIGATION SYSTEM THAT RECEIVES SIGNALS FROM SATELLITES OVERHEAD, LOCATING THE CAR ON ITS OWN ROUTE MAP.

TURN RIGHT FOR CLEAR WATER LAKE

SPEED LIMIT 20 MPH

2:54 ARRIVAL

The Road Ahead

Most serious car crashes happen because drivers make mistakes. The aim of driverless cars is to make road travel safer, so that traffic flows and accidents hardly ever happen, but we still have a long way to go! First, these cars must learn to identify everything in a car's path correctly, and make instant decisions. Another risk is that a car's computer system may be **hacked** and the communication system blocked.

ROBO-DOC

Every year, millions of people have surgery that is performed not by a human but by a robot. A team of doctors and nurses control the robotic surgeon at all times. Under their supervision, the robot makes exact movements, cutting and stitching precisely and safely.

PRECISION WORK

The robot can slide a surgical instrument into a cut that is only 1 to 2 centimetres long. A human surgeon needs more room to move and must make a longer cut, which creates a bigger wound and means more stitches.

STITCHING UP

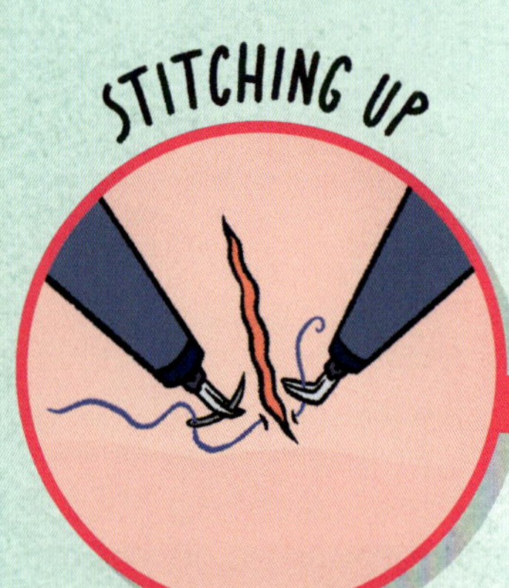

This surgical robot has four arms, fitted with different **end effectors.**

Camera

The patient lies on an operating table, which can be raised or lowered to exactly the right height.

SURGICAL TOOLS

A robotic surgeon uses a variety of instruments. The end effectors on the robot arms are small surgical tools, which fit easily inside the patient's body.

HOT LASER

A laser is used to remove diseased tissue.

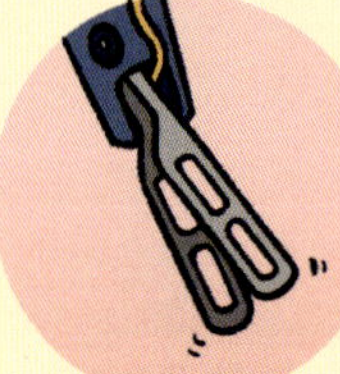

PINCERS

Pincers hold tiny nerves and blood vessels.

SCALPEL

A razor-sharp scalpel makes fine, precise cuts.

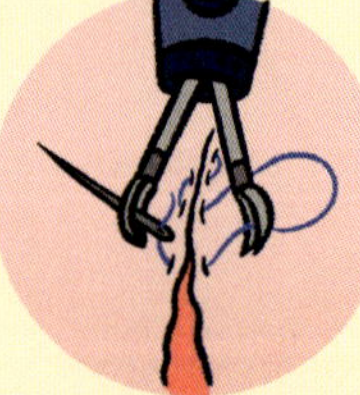

NEEDLES

Fine needles stitch wounds after surgery.

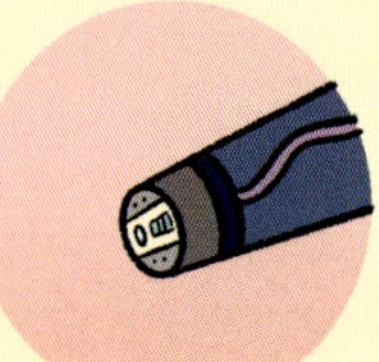

CAMERA

An endoscope has lenses, to see inside the patient.

Autonomous Surgery

Robotic surgeons are very good at doing the same thing over and over again – their stitching is excellent! In the future, an AI may control robot surgeons some of the time (without a human controller), and they may be able to learn through experience.

HUMAN SUPERVISION

A team of specialist doctors and nurses stays with the patient during the surgery, making sure the patient is comfortable. The nurse swaps the tools and instruments on the robot arms, and checks the robot is working properly.

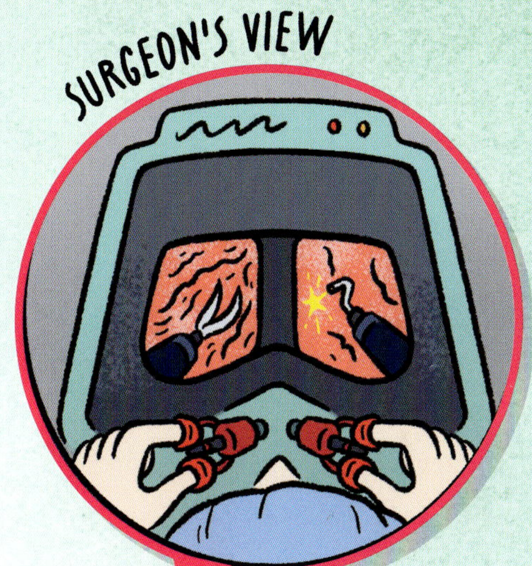

INSIDE VIEW

Cameras and lights at the end of one of the robot's arms allow the surgical team to see what's happening inside the patient's body. The surgeon guides the tools on the other arms, to operate on the patient.

CONSOLE CONNECT

The surgeon controls the tools using a console that is connected to the Internet. In some hospitals, cutting-edge VR (virtual reality) headsets have replaced consoles.

Nurse

Console

Looking through the viewer, the surgeon can see what the robot's camera sees.

The surgeon uses the controllers to move each robot arm. The robot translates these movements into micro adjustments.

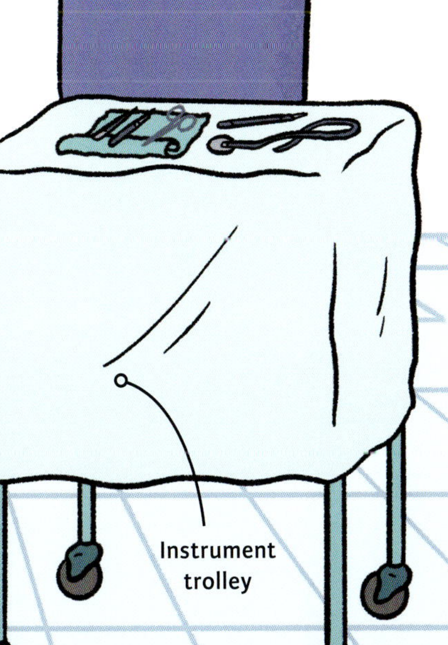

UNDERWATER ROBOT

The deep, dark ocean is a place few of us will ever visit, let alone live and work. We send robots instead! Robotic arms equipped with tools snake their way through the water. These deep-sea robots travel long distances, building and repairing broken machinery at depth.

DEEP-SEA DIVER

Underwater robots explore the seabed, mapping the ocean floor, fixing communication cables, and repairing oil rigs. The robot is built from several sections or modules, which are connected by flexible joints, allowing the robot to bend and wriggle around obstacles.

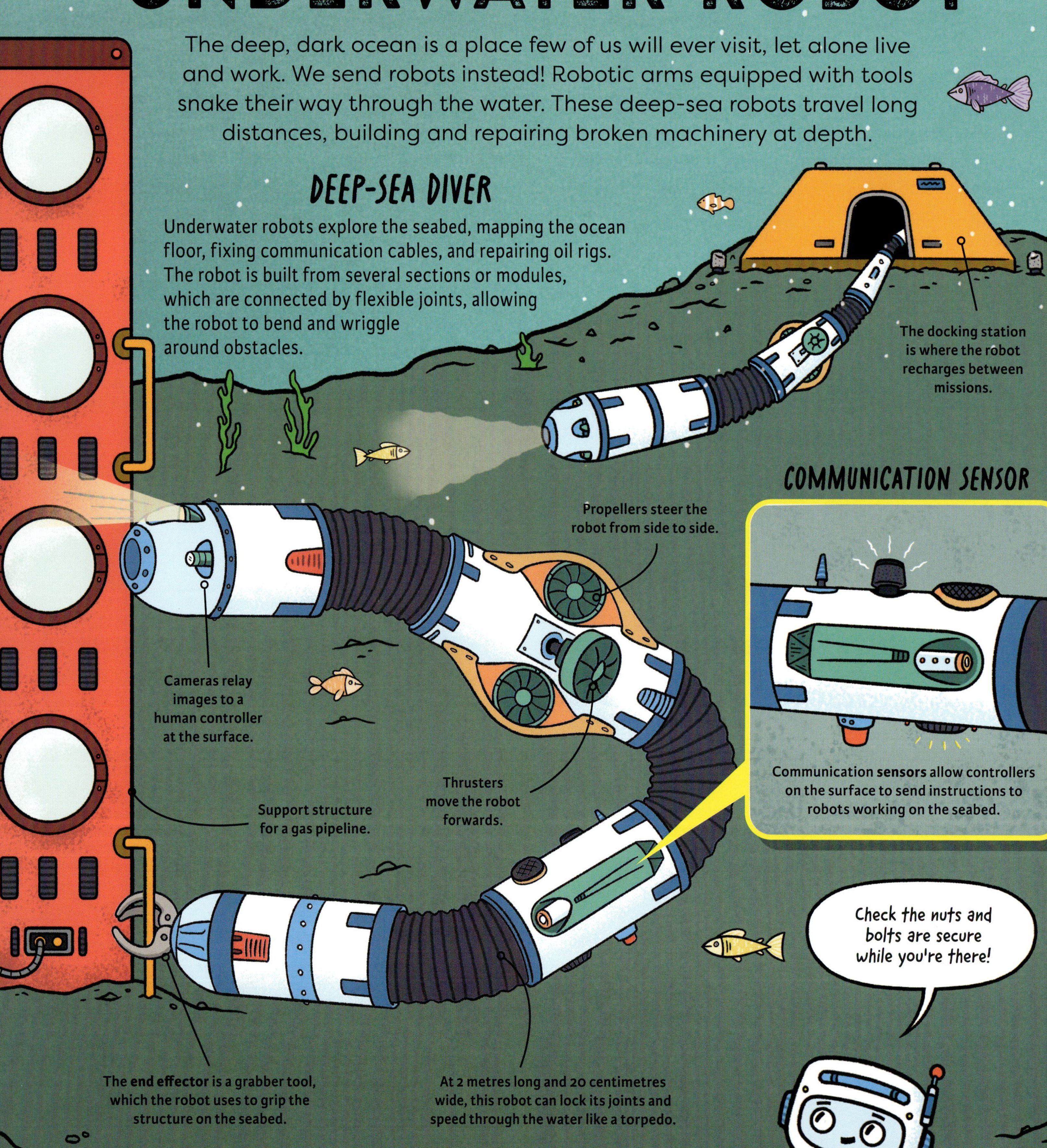

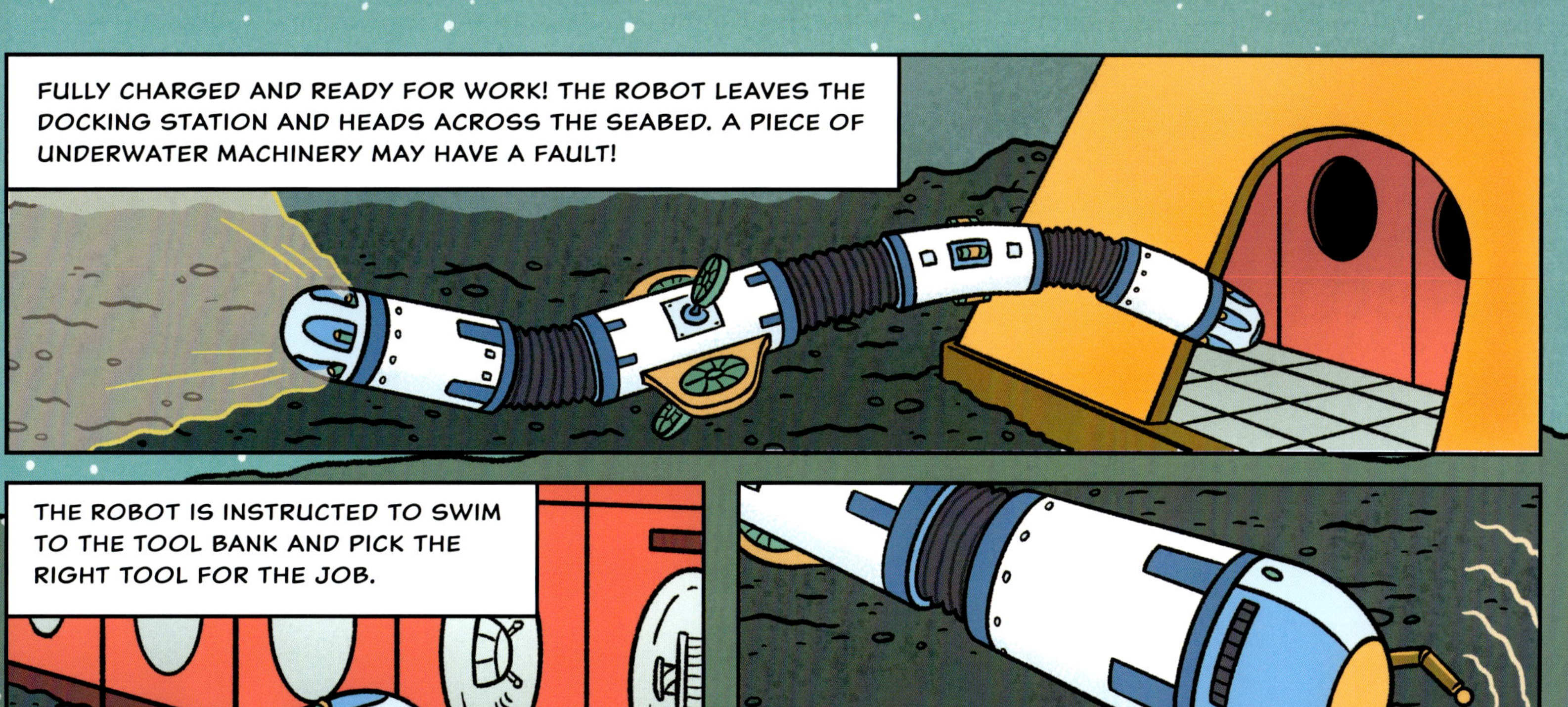

Biomimicry

Some undersea robots are flexible, twisting and turning sideways like fish as they move through water. Designing robots and machines that mimic animal movements and body shapes is called biomimicry.

A jellyfish robot has a soft, bell-shaped body. It can float in one place, taking measurements or observing endangered ocean habitats.

A kangaroo robot hops along on its bouncy back legs and helps us to understand balance and advanced leg movement. As its legs bend, they make enough electricity to power the next jump.

This crab-like robot is so small it could pass through the eye of a needle! Robots like this travel into tiny spaces no other machine or human being could ever reach.

ROBOT ROVER

Exploring other planets is dangerous for human beings. We can't survive the freezing temperatures, the radiation from the Sun, or the lack of oxygen - but robots can!

EARTH TO MARS

Robotic rovers on Mars study the red rocks and conduct experiments, while searching for water and signs of ancient alien life. Scientists on Earth decide what the rover should investigate.

Two Navcams, or navigation cameras, work like a pair of eyes to 'see' the landscape. Controllers on Earth use them to plot a safe route for the rover.

The mast carries cameras and scanners to observe the landscape.

Antenna

Weather station and wind sensors

Power pack

INSIDE THE POWER PACK

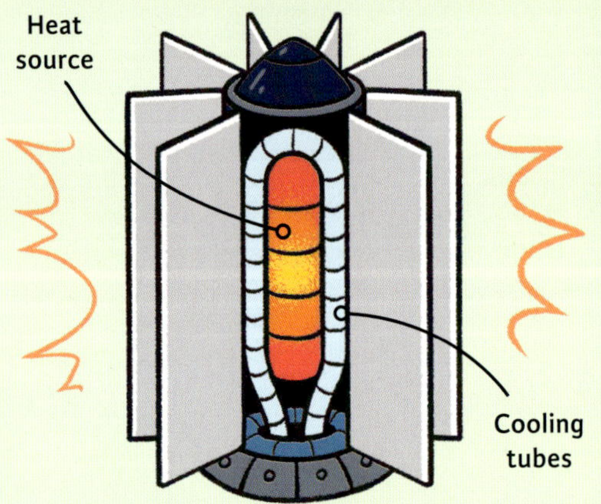

The rover has a power pack that uses heat given out by radioactive fuel to make electricity. It's like a mini nuclear power station, with enough fuel inside to last for many years.

The rover has six springy aluminium wheels that clamber up and over huge Martian rocks.

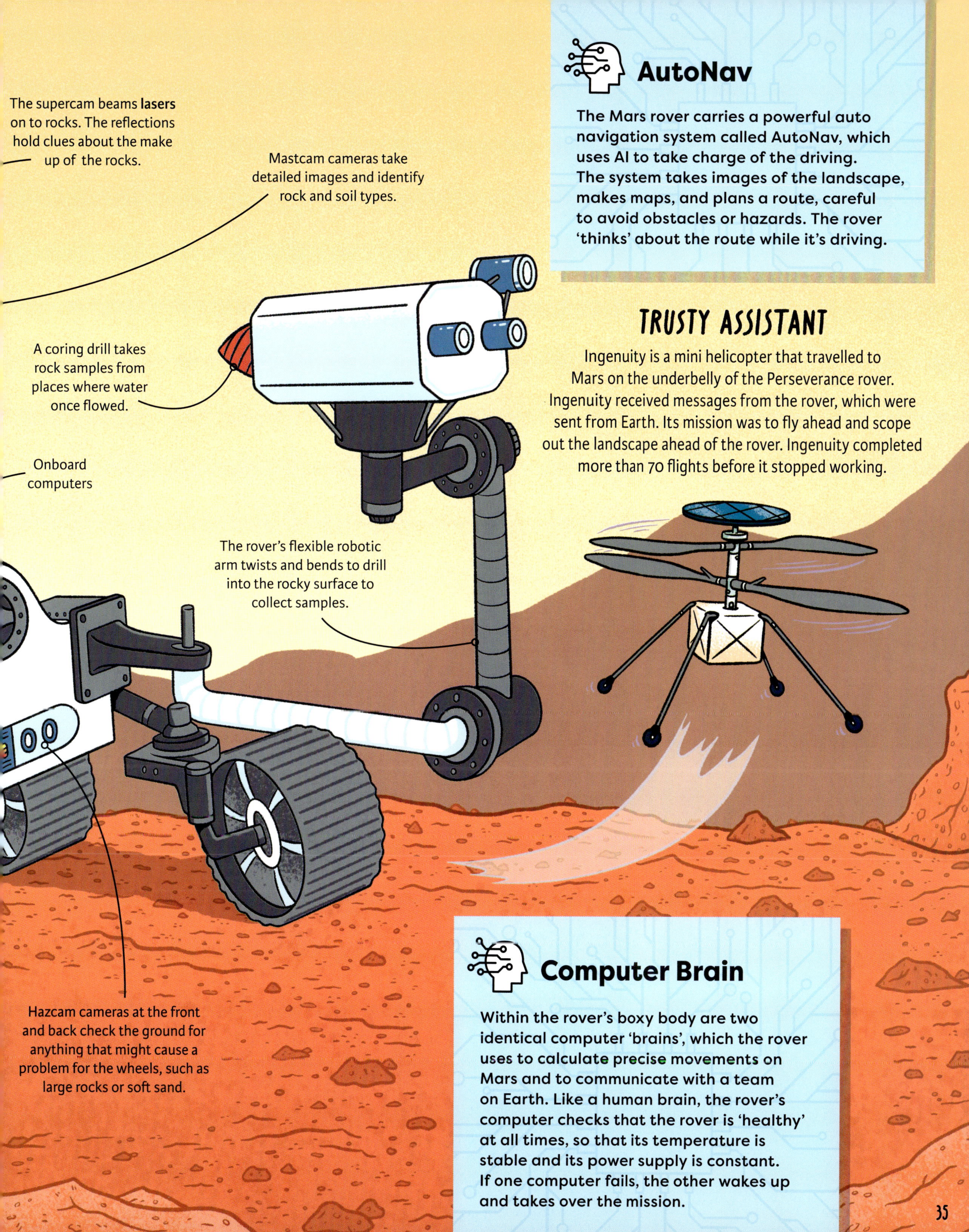

AutoNav

The Mars rover carries a powerful auto navigation system called AutoNav, which uses AI to take charge of the driving. The system takes images of the landscape, makes maps, and plans a route, careful to avoid obstacles or hazards. The rover 'thinks' about the route while it's driving.

TRUSTY ASSISTANT

Ingenuity is a mini helicopter that travelled to Mars on the underbelly of the Perseverance rover. Ingenuity received messages from the rover, which were sent from Earth. Its mission was to fly ahead and scope out the landscape ahead of the rover. Ingenuity completed more than 70 flights before it stopped working.

Computer Brain

Within the rover's boxy body are two identical computer 'brains', which the rover uses to calculate precise movements on Mars and to communicate with a team on Earth. Like a human brain, the rover's computer checks that the rover is 'healthy' at all times, so that its temperature is stable and its power supply is constant. If one computer fails, the other wakes up and takes over the mission.

GAME ON!

Robots and other computer-powered machines are very good at following a set of rules, which makes them great at games like chess. Building world-class chess computers was a big step towards creating artificial intelligence. Today's top chess computers can beat any chess champion, but it wasn't always that way...

Minimax

Chess AIs use an **algorithm** called Minimax to look at all possible moves. At each turn, the AI says to itself, 'How can I minimise my chances of losing, when my opponent is trying to maximise their chances of winning?'. The more moves ahead an AI (or a person!) can see, the better their chances are of winning.

Who wants a match?

A chess computer that is programmed with the rules of the game can play against a human. To beat a chess champion, a chess computer needs to use **artificial intelligence**. A human moves the chess pieces for the AI.

Early chess computers were too slow to look very far ahead. Top chess champions could always figure out a way to beat them.

Why are computers so slow?

Here's how you should play your next move.

A chess AI can learn clever ways to start and end games from chess champions. But this type of AI cannot actually learn for itself.

To figure out many possible moves all at once, a chess AI needs a very fast processor. In 1997, a chess computer called Deep Blue beat the Russian world champion, Garry Kasparov, in six games.

Playing against a chess master, a chess AI thinks as many as 20 moves ahead. It searches through billions of different ways the game might be played, looking for the move that is most likely to lead to a win.

Today's chess AIs are much better at playing chess than humans (and some people use them to cheat!), but that's just the beginning. Developing chess AIs has taught us how to build smarter machines that predict the weather, tailor medicines to individuals, and revolutionise the way we do science.

Chess Engines

Modern AIs do not even need to be taught how to play chess. They play themselves millions of times, using **artificial neural networks** to learn which moves are good to play. Every win reinforces their knowledge. Pretty soon, they are amazing! This is called **machine learning,** and it is helping other types of AIs and robots to learn for themselves.

HOW TO TEACH A ROBOT

How do you teach a robot to do its job? You could program it, writing step-by-step instructions and rules for it to follow. Or, you could train it using lots of **data,** so that it can learn the rules itself and make its own decisions. This is called **machine learning**.

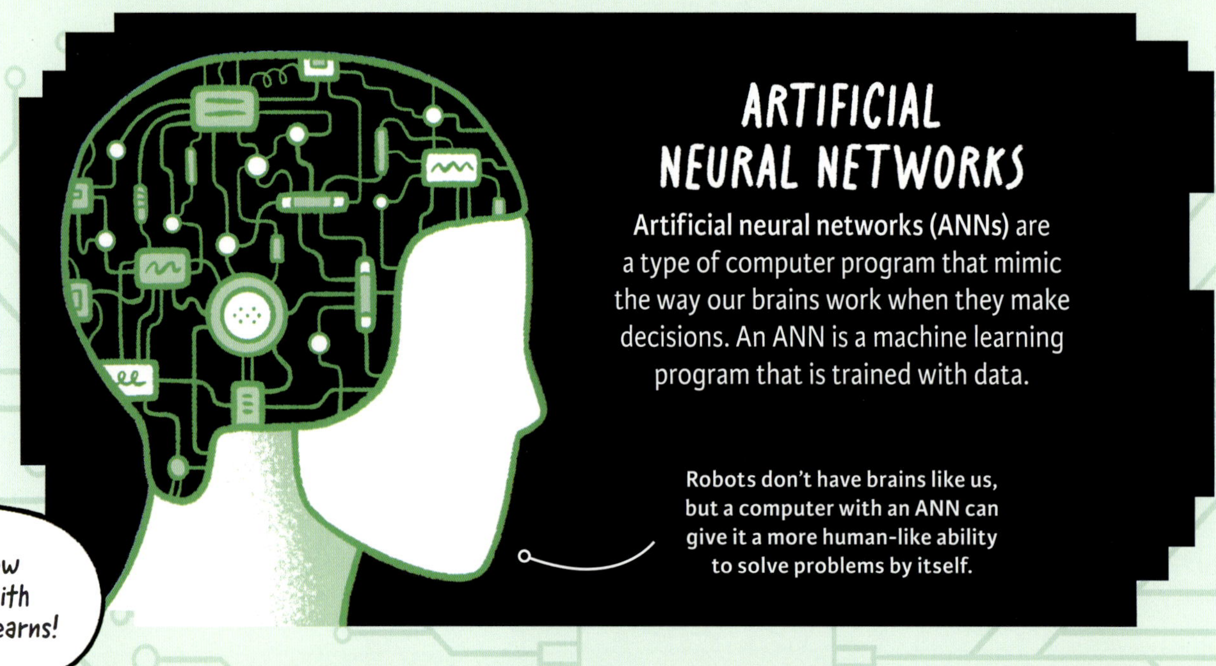

ARTIFICIAL NEURAL NETWORKS

Artificial neural networks (ANNs) are a type of computer program that mimic the way our brains work when they make decisions. An ANN is a machine learning program that is trained with data.

Robots don't have brains like us, but a computer with an ANN can give it a more human-like ability to solve problems by itself.

This is how a robot with onboard AI learns!

PREDICTING THE ANSWER

An ANN is trained with data, so that it gets better at predicting the answers to questions. It can still get things wrong. The more data used and the bigger the ANN, the greater the confidence you can have in its answers. Voice assistants use ANNs to learn how to answer your questions.

Are you sure it will rain today?

I'm 60 per cent positive.

Machine learning enables AI-equipped technologies to respond to commands and questions.

MACHINE LEARNING

Huge amounts of data is used to train an AI to produce more accurate responses to questions, or to make the actions a robot takes more successful. There are three main types of machine learning:

1 SUPERVISED

An AI is trained using data that has already been labelled, by a computer program or by humans. These correct labels are used to automatically 'supervise' the AI's predictions and adjust its settings to improve accuracy. When it's trained, the AI can label new images all by itself!

2 UNSUPERVISED

An AI is given lots of unlabelled data and organises it into groups that share similarities, all by itself. This is good for discovering hidden patterns.

Pictures with brown dogs

Pictures with grey dogs

3 REINFORCEMENT

The AI learns by trial and error whether an action is successful or not. Correct actions are rewarded, which enables a robot to learn which actions have successful outcomes.

Problems With AI

If the data used to train an AI is unbalanced and doesn't reflect reality well, it can lead to incorrect predictions. This is known as bias. When humans label training data for AI it can also cause bias.

This dog is disqualified from the show because the AI's training data didn't contain pictures of poodles.

ARTISTIC ROBOTS?

Robots can do all kinds of jobs, but could added **AI** help them to be artists? We've seen how **machine learning** and **artificial neural networks** (ANNs) can enable an AI to add text labels to images. However, this can also be reversed, so an AI can use a text prompt to generate an image.

AI ART

We can train a **generative AI** to create pictures by getting two ANNs to compete against each other. One of the ANNs is called the Generator. Its job is to turn a text description into a new picture. Another ANN, called the Discriminator, compares the generated picture with real ones. If it spots a fake picture, it wins. Otherwise, the Generator wins.

GENERATOR

I'll beat the Discriminator this time!

The Generator has been trained to link words to pictures. It has a basic model of a bunny rabbit stored, which it uses to generate a picture. Each time it does this, it adds random changes, so the pictures are always slightly different.

3 GENERATED IMAGE

output

1 TEXT PROMPT

Tell the AI what picture to create.

A bunny rabbit

input

input

2 NOISE

An image of **white noise** is used as the raw material for the Generator to turn into the picture.

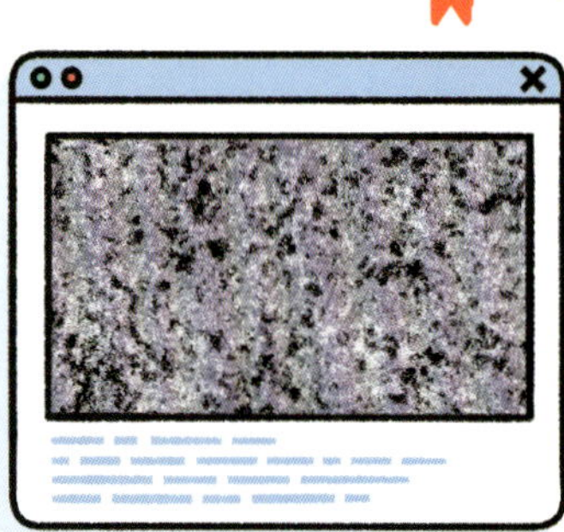

Can you tell the difference between real images and AI images? It's not always easy.

REAL PICTURES

The Discriminator has been trained with real images that match the text prompt, so it can tell the difference between real images and generated ones.

Bunny rabbit

Bunny rabbit

Bunny rabbit

input

FAKES

If the Discriminator finds bunnies with three ears, five legs or rainbow coloured fur, the Generator fails the forgery test!

output

DISCRIMINATOR

input

How do we know if the Generator's image of a bunny looks right? We get the Discriminator to check it!

output

6

REAL

Success! The Generator's image of a bunny looks so real that even the Discriminator could not spot the difference.

AI GENERATED VIDEO

To create a video with moving pictures, the AI generates thousands of still images and then plays them back in order. It's like a very clever flipbook!

Real or Fake?

A **deepfake** is a video or image made by AI that shows a real person (usually someone famous), but the things they are doing and saying are completely made up. Sometimes details or sudden changes can give you a clue that what you are looking at is a fake.

CHATBOTS

A chatbot is an **AI** program that interacts with humans, using language to have a conversation. Chatbots respond to written or spoken questions, and can write detailed reports on all kinds of subjects. Many chatbots are accessed using websites or smartphone apps. They are being used to make robots smarter, too.

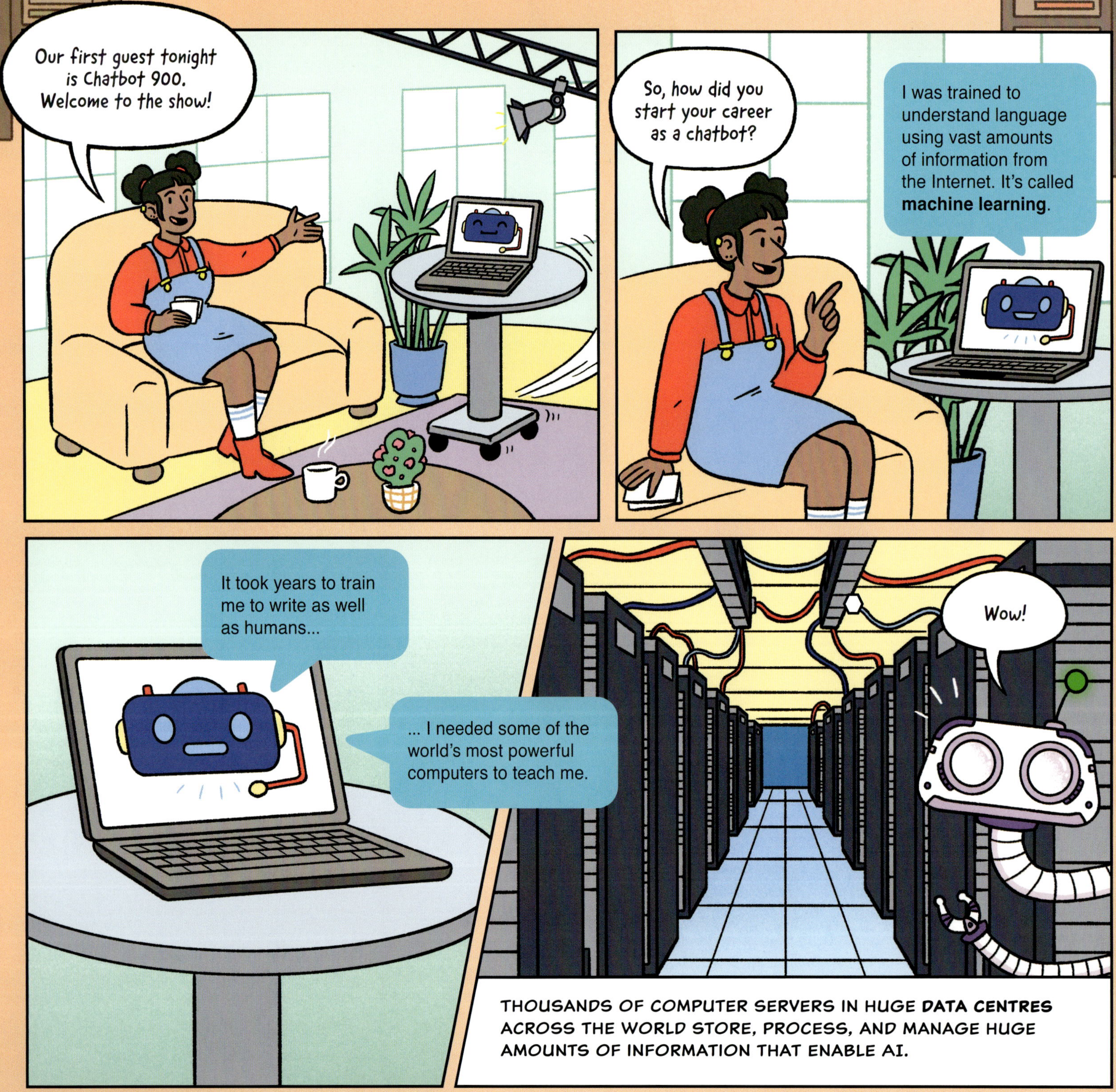

It took years to train me to write as well as humans...

... I needed some of the world's most powerful computers to teach me.

Wow!

THOUSANDS OF COMPUTER SERVERS IN HUGE **DATA CENTRES** ACROSS THE WORLD STORE, PROCESS, AND MANAGE HUGE AMOUNTS OF INFORMATION THAT ENABLE AI.

Chatbots sound convincing, but you don't always guess the correct answer, do you?

No. But chatbots are much better than predictive text on a smart phone.

THE SAME **GENERATIVE AI** CAN BE USED TO CREATE IMAGES AND VIDEOS.

Generative AI

A chatbot doesn't search for existing information: it makes up its own responses. This is called **generative AI** because it generates new content. A chatbot can use language so well that it appears to know a lot, but it cannot understand what it says. Large Language Models can be trained on images, videos, and audio, as well as text. Generative AI can also learn from how people move, and then use that information to help humanoid robots move more like us.

SUPERCOMPUTING

Robot control and AI are only possible thanks to immense computer power called supercomputing, where we link clusters of computers together to work as a team. The units carry out complex calculations at high speed. The largest clusters, or supercomputers, have millions of these smaller units. All of this computer power is needed to train AI chatbots and control driverless cars.

AI using supercomputing can look for new medicines. In the past, scientists spent a long time searching for chemicals that might cure a disease. Most did not work. AI can check things much faster, by imagining new chemicals to see what they can do.
Quantum computer
This is a new kind of computer that one day might be able to do certain kinds of maths faster than any normal computer. A quantum computer does not use ordinary microchips and at the moment needs to operate at very very cold temperatures: -272°C! There are a lot of problems to solve before a quantum computer is reliable enough for everyday use, but perhaps in the future we'll all have a quantum supercomputer in our homes.
Today, a lot of criminals try to steal money from people online. There are billions of people online each day, so it is hard to spot the criminals. An AI using supercomputing can search for strange patterns and ask for more checks. It is getting harder and harder to cheat online, thanks to AI!
Scientists are working out how to make electricity with nuclear fusion. This is the way the Sun makes its heat and light. The problem is that fusion is very hard to control. So, scientists are using AI to build a system that can keep the fusion running long enough to produce energy.

GLOSSARY

Actuator A part of a robot that produces movements.

Algorithm A set of step-by-step instructions given to a computer or person telling them how to complete a task.

Artificial intelligence The ability of a computer or robot to do jobs that are normally left to humans.

Artifical Neural Network (ANN) A computer programme that mimics the neural networks in our brains, to enable computers to learn like us. They are one form of machine learning.

Autonomous When something is in charge of itself.

Axis of movement An imaginary line around which a mechanical joint rotates.

Biomimicry When a machine is designed to imitate the body of a living thing.

Data Facts and figures that are used to analyse and make decisions. When information can be processed by a computer or AI, it is called computer data.

Data centre A place where large numbers of computers are stored, which hold data being used by people all over the world.

Deepfake when AI is used to create videos or pictures that seem real, but they are fake. It may show someone doing or saying something that never actually happened.

Drone A robot vehicle that moves around by itself or under remote control. Mostly drones are flying machines but could move on land or water as well.

Electrode An electrical sensor, often used within a medical device.

End effector A tool used by a robot to do its job. A gripper is one kind of end effector.

Exoskeleton A robotic suit that a person wears to help them move and be faster and stronger.

Generative AI (Gen-AI) A type of AI that is able to create new things autonomously. It produces original text, images and audio without copying them from earlier versions, and without help from humans.

Global Positioning System (GPS) A navigation system that uses signals from satellites to show where you are.

Hacking When a person or a computer programme takes over another computer without asking.

Hydraulics A mechanical system that uses fluids to push pistons and create movement.

Large Language Model (LLM) A system used by AI to understand language.

Lidar Standing for Light Detection and Ranging, this scanner uses light rays to build up detailed maps of what is in an area.

Machine learning A system for training AIs to do a job.

Mech suit A robotic suit that is worn on part or all of the body and is controlled by the wearer. The control system synchronises with the wearer's movements. It's also called an exoskeleton.

Nanobot A tiny robot measuring only a few millionths of a metre.

Neural network A set of nerves connected in the brain. ANNs used in machine learning copy this natural system.

Piston A pump-like system used in hydraulics that creates a pushing force by using liquids pumped into a sealed tube.

Prosthetic An artificial body part.

Remote operated vehicle (ROV) Another name for a drone, especially one that works underwater.

Radioactive When a substance has unstable atoms that fall apart and give out energy.

Robot A machine that may be controlled by a computer (autonomous) or by a human. Robots come in different shapes and sizes. Most are designed to do specific tasks but they can be reprogrammed to do different tasks. Some robots look a bit like people, but most do not. They can 'see' their environment, make decisions and move on their own.

Satellite Something that orbits a larger object, like a planet. Artificial satellites are used for communication, navigation and many other jobs.

Sensor A device that detects and measures something.

Sonar Short for Sound Navigation and Ranging, this system bounces sounds off objects. These echoes tell us how big and far away the object is. Sonar is especially useful underwater.

Stepper motor An electric motor that can move in very small steps one by one so it turns in very precise amounts. Robotic arms used stepper motors for this reason.

INDEX